GIRL, LET THAT SH*T GO!

GIRL, LET THAT SH*T GO!

Empowering Women to Get Through Toxic Relationships, Take Back Their Power & Own Their Badassery

ASHLEY BURNEY

Copyright © 2021 by Ashley Burney

All rights reserved. No part of this book may be reproduced in any manner whatsoever without written permission except in the case of brief quotations embodied in critical articles and reviews.

First Printing, 2021

Contents

Dedication — vii

Disclaimer — 1

Foreword
Down Bad — 4

Chapter 1
Let That Shit Go — 7

Chapter 2
Familial Trauma — 14

Chapter 3
Young and Inexperienced — 19

Chapter 4
Mind Control — 27

Chapter 5
Pressure Doesn't Always Make Diamonds — 31

Chapter 6
Situationships — 38

Chapter 7
Hurt People, Hurt People — 43

Chapter 8
In Denial — 50

Chapter 9
Strangers — 57

Chapter 10
See the Signs												65

Chapter 11
Get Your Life											74

Chapter 12
Toxic Masculinity										79

Chapter 13
Fear													85

The Tipping Point
														93

Chapter 14
Taking Back the Key										94

Chapter 15
Accountability											103

Chapter 16
Love After All											110

Until We Meet Again
You Get to Write the Next Chapter						117

Acknowledgements
														121

To Trenna and Tray,
Thanks for showing me what a homegrown love looks like.

Disclaimer

Before reading this book, it is helpful to note that I speak candidly and use a ton of profanity. You will laugh in some instances, cry in others, shout out "Girl, yes!" in other instances or just plain be quiet when the tea is served a little too hot. Understand that it's all in service of you. This book is not for the faint of heart, but rather for those who are working endlessly to heal their hearts. This book is not for the grammar nazis either. To be honest, as long as you get the message, it doesn't matter how it's received. I speak to you from a place of love. I speak to you authentically and unapologetically. You deserve that.

> **FOR ALL THE WOMEN OUT THERE DEVALUING THEMSELVES FOR FUCK BOYS WITH APARTMENTS INFESTED WITH ROACHES AND DEEP ROOTED ISSUES THEY HAVE YET TO HEAL FROM.**
> **THIS IS FOR YOU.**
> **LET THAT SHIT GO!**

Girl, let that shit go! Stop lowering the bar for yourself. Stop allowing toxic men to diminish your sense of self worth. Stop allowing other people's survival mechanisms to dictate your own sense of value and purpose. Stop beating yourself up for giving way too much and accepting way too little. Stop treating your heart like a liability. Let that shit go.

It is not a bad thing to love. It is not a bad thing to share your heart. It's not a bad thing to open up and be vulnerable. You matter.

Your heart is full and pure and precious like rubies. If someone doesn't understand this, it is NOT your job to convince them or try to prove how valuable you are. Listen, Babe, you are a bad ass fucking goddess who's up to some great things in your life and you don't need anyone or anything standing in the way of your purpose. Let that shit go.

Realize that what's within you, no man nor woman can take. You deserve the best and if it doesn't work out, that says nothing about who you are but rather it says that that person doesn't match the vision for what you're doing in your life. You've got some big things happening in the near future. This thing you're experiencing is *real* and it *stings*. Know that this too shall pass.

Things didn't work out? It's okay. You're not responsible for other people's energy or their shit, but what you ARE responsible for is how you allow that energy or shit to rub off on you. So what are you going to do? What's next? We've got shifts, breakthroughs and transformation to experience. You're allowed to be with the heartache, but you get to decide how you plan to use that to move forward. Your life is in your hands.

This is your journey.

Foreword

Down Bad

A low point in your life when all the morals and logic you usually have goes right out the window

Whew Chile, I met this man on a dating app. We had spoken a few times and when the "time was right" we decided to meet. I had gotten brunch drunk earlier in the day and was feeling adventurous, so I said, fuck it, I'll go meet this guy. We met for ice cream and then went on a low level hike. On our walk down the mountain the clouds had suddenly turned grey. The sky was this deep blue black color, the thunder rumbled low in the distance and what started as a low drizzle turned into a full out downpour. We kept on walking, allowing the rain to beat down on our skin and soak our clothes. All the while laughing because, fuck it's a hot summer day, was rain even in the forecast? By the time we made it back to our cars, we were drenched in sweat and water. He gave me a hand towel and we sat in his car and talked for another half hour until the rain stopped. He didn't even care about messing up the seats in his car and that carefree energy piqued my interest.

The first time I went to his house, I looked past all of the mess. When we entered, it was dark. We went up to the attic and we hung out in this messy room. There were boxes and clothes everywhere, no sheets on the bed. Man listen, that room was a full out shit storm! I wasn't ready to go home, so I stayed over, we had sex and I left around 6am. Come to think of it, I had a few drinks before I came over that night, as it was the 4th of July and I had just finished hanging with my cousins. Needless to say he was a rebound for me. I had been emotionally attached to another man I was trying to let go of and was feeling the aftermath, and he recently had gotten out of a relationship; we filled a gap for each other.

As we grew closer, I learned that we were never really alone. This apartment was heavily infested with roaches. YES! ROACHES! There was a host of them greeting us on the steps as we entered the apartment. There would be roaches trying (and sometimes succeeding) to shower with us. Never saw any in the bed thankfully, but they were all over the place. He pretended not to see them, and I was too afraid to speak up and address it for fear of hurting his feelings. As if we were not literally in Joe's Apartment (movie reference) with the only thing missing being the flying ones. I was downnnn bad, bih! I looked past all of the extra critters because he had been through some mess. I looked past all of it because the sex was great. I looked past it all because I felt like he was in a space of really starting to let his guard down. His feeling of unworthiness fueled my feelings of unworthiness. Then he ghosted my ass. This mu'fucka with the roach infested apartment ghosted *me*.

He was a well dressed, seemingly put together shitbag. Him ghosting me was the biggest honor, because I settled so hard with him. I knew he was still harboring depressed feelings over his ex. I knew he felt like he didn't deserve to be with a woman as good as me, because he said it often. I for damn sure knew that I deserved better than dick and roaches. A person can have such pretty packaging, but if it's shit underneath, eventually, it will begin to reek everywhere. He had a host of insecurities and he wore them like a badge of honor. It rubbed off on me. Being ghosted is horrible, but what's even worse is making someone else's insecurities, inconsistencies and shortcomings mean something about you.

Before you go judging me for being down bad, understand that some of you reading this book are down bad too. It just looks a different way. That's alright though sis, we gonna get it together. By the end of this book, you will step fully into your healing. Owning every damn bit of your magic and never having to worry about being in that deep hole ever again, and if you do get there, you'll be more prepared with the tools to get out faster.

Heartache hurts like hell and being ghosted is about one of the worst things to experience. However, what's even worse is allowing the bullshit to take you out. After that experience, I vowed to never let one person's shit become my own. I vowed to not carry that energy into my next relationship. I vowed to truly heal and **see** myself. As a result, now we are here embarking on this journey together. Snapping out of the bullshit and letting shit go. So if there's nothing else you've learned from me. Hear this:

Let. That. Shit. Go.

Chapter 1

Let That Shit Go

If a person doesn't want to be in your life, it is not your business to find out why

My Story:

He was my everything. I worshipped the ground he walked on and in my eyes he could do no wrong. We spent time together and took so many road trips, I lost count. He told me he loved me often. I was his baby. There was nothing anyone could say about me, because he'd be the first one to defend me. He showed up. He was there whenever I needed him. He was just...perfect. Until he wasn't. When I finally took the rose colored glasses off and saw him in his imperfection, I was devastated. I realized what those road trips actually consisted of and my picture perfect image of him became distorted. The glass, permanently stained. A scarlet letter etched in his heart. There were many women. I could probably name each of them one by one. It was a constant violation. The lies. The deceit... How could the first example of what a man should be and how a woman should be treated by a man, be the one to pull the wool right before my eyes? How could this "perfect" man turn out to be the very man that I would encounter at various points throughout my life? How could he do my mom like that, but more importantly, how could he expose ME, his little girl, to all of this?

Those perfect road trips back and forth to New Jersey and North Carolina only served as a cover up for the pain he was inflicting on my mother. And I, an oblivious accomplice. Despite the infidelities, he was there for his children up until he and my mom had split. The divorce was the catalyst for years of mistrust that I would embody within myself and toward men. I come from a big family, being the youngest of 6 children growing up in a house together. After the divorce, three of my older siblings were forced to make their own way in the world by finding somewhere else to live. I can't even begin to imagine the pain and betrayal they felt. Knowing that one of the only consistent homes they've ever known would be ripped from under them. That they would have to learn the hard way how to navigate an already difficult world. They didn't deserve that. With the way we grew up, we were no strangers to adversity, but that wasn't our burden to carry.

I wanted to believe that our father would show up for us...show up for ME. I wanted to believe that despite the separation I would always be his baby...his little girl...his princess. Needless to say, all of that changed. He had another child with the sidechick, a woman who was the daughter of one of his closest friends. Just as he didn't protect me, her father didn't protect her. His leaving led to me feeling replaced, betrayed and worst of all unworthy. He had a new shiny thing to take care of. There was no longer any room for me. He had a new child to idolize him. A new child to ruin. A new child to bear the weight of a world too chaotic than he deserved. A world where he grew up and internalized that feeling of scum, unworthiness, rejection. This internalization manifested into a life full of no direction, perpetuating child molestation, crime and hurt. He tried to take his own life more than once, and he now walks the world as a victim, expecting the world to raise him because my father failed as a man. Yet in my brother's eyes, my father can do no wrong. In his eyes, my father is perfectly imperfect. In his eyes, our father is king, even though he robs him of his disability money every chance he gets since he lives in an Assisted Living Facility. My father, probably feeling like he deserves it for the years of neglect and pain inflicted, sweeps it all under the rug. My brother, his shiny new baby. Never grappling with the fact that he fucked him up too.

It took me 20 years to forgive him. I was angry for so long, and I searched for him in every encounter I had with a man. I constantly judged myself. Thinking that I was either too much or not enough. I developed a mindset that men always leave, because he left. As a result, I loved a little too hard and held on a little too tight. I felt like no matter what I did or how much I gave of myself in relationships, eventually they too, wouldn't think my love was enough and would leave. I treated my heart like a liability. I internalized a false narrative that loving someone or sharing my heart was a bad thing. I struggled with the story of unworthiness, wearing it as if it were permanently branded onto my skin with a rusty steel rod, and it showed up everywhere. Namely in the form of me being afraid to trust myself, own my power, take up space and being viciously afraid of my own greatness and light.

It wasn't until I released the burden, learned the power of forgiveness and accepted my healing process that I began to see so much more possibility. My father loves me to death. I'm sure he had a lot of reasons for why he couldn't be as present as he wanted to. I now understand that he simply didn't know any better. He had a mother who enabled him and never held him accountable for his actions. My grandfather (as much as I adore him, may he rest in peace) perpetuated the same messages of unworthiness down to me unintentionally by comparing me to my Nurse sister and telling me that there was no money to be generated as a Life Coach. Here was another man I love telling me I was worthless. He did the same thing to my grandmother in the sense of cheating on her and exposing his children to it. All of his kids knew he was cheating because they, too, had been to the women's houses. This type of trauma gets passed down from generation to generation, but who is going to break that shit? We can go on and choose victimhood by blaming and shaming and asking all of the why questions. The answers may never come. Acknowledge it. Me not having access to these answers doesn't serve me anymore. It's not personal. It simply isn't my business and that's the most liberating thing to know. You get to decide to be the one to end the generational trauma and heal. I hope you choose healing.

I used to say that I was a broken girl with daddy issues. I now know that's not true. The truth is I was never broken to begin with. There's often this misconception that people are broken and need to be fixed or that they are lost and need to be found. The reality is that you are exactly where you're supposed to be in your process and you are a whole and complete person. Sure, there are good and questionable aspects of us all, but if we only focus on the questionable aspects and make that mean everything about our existence, we miss out on the parts that are absolutely beautiful. Honey, it's all beautiful. The way your face scrunches up when you think to yourself, "This mutha fucka really tried it!" The way your nose flares up when you're so angry that you can't even put into words the level of pissivity that exists on the inside. When your mind is at ease and you're experiencing total bliss when you see the look on your baby's face as they engage in sheer and utter unorchestrated play. When you're having a full belly laugh to the point of tears and your stomach hurts. When you're just sitting silent, doing nothing but being your whole ass, poppin ass self. You, my dear, are as beautiful as they come. Embrace it all because it makes you who you are. You are complete. You are free.

I've had conversations with women who've had absentee fathers. The consistency in truth telling comes down to this: We are all searching…reaching…craving…crying…dying…to truly know what love is. To experience what it means to be loved correctly by a partner. Understand this: WE teach people how to treat us. WE teach them what's acceptable. WE teach them what's unacceptable. WE often downgrade because within us we don't feel like we deserve it. A part of us is still that little girl searching for her father. Wondering if he ever loved her at all. Wondering if we'll ever be good enough for anyone. Remember that the goal is not to be good enough for anyone, but to honor and dig deep within your own inner magic and realize that you've always been enough. **As you are.** Anyone who chooses not to be a part of your story is missing out, NOT you. What you bring to the table is so unique and special. So original and precious. You deserve someone who wants to be there. It is not your job to try and keep or hold them. Anyone who wants to walk out of your life was never intended to be there long term.

There's a clip from Tyler Perry's play "Madea Goes to Jail" where Madea addresses a gentleman who was heartbroken because his wife had walked out on him and was cheating with his best friend. Madea says, "If someone wants to walk out of your life, let them go. Especially if you know you [have] done everything you can do. You done sat around and been the best man or the best woman you can be and they still wanna go, let [th]em go. Whatever they running after, they'll see what they had in a minute but by then it's gonna be too late." Whether your heartbreak is over your father or over the person who has repeatedly shown you in multiple ways that they don't want you, they'll realize what they had. However, you'll be long gone giving and receiving that good loving from the one who always knew. So don't get caught up in the why's or the how's. It's not important. It's not personal. It's not your business.

A Practice:

Using the space below, write a list of all the people, events or circumstances in your life that you're choosing to let go of simply because they don't deserve a place in your life. Give a few words to thoughts, feelings, or body sensations that you're choosing to be done with. When you're done, scribble all up and down that mutha fucka! Get creative and draw over it if it suits you. Hell, add color if you want. Your pain doesn't have to be ugly anymore. It's beautiful. You got through it. What's done is done. The damage has already run its course. It's over, and the choice to remove the deadweight is in your hands this time.

An Affirmation:

Today I let go of...

I choose to replace this with...

I am...

> *What you choose to release no longer has a hold on you.*
> *Set yourself free, Babe.*

Chapter 2

Familial Trauma

Some Wounds Cut Deep

Her Story:

My first heartbreak was caused by my parents. I was raised solely by my mother. My mother had my siblings and I very young, so unfortunately she was a child raising multiple children. My mother never came from a strong support system, and in turn that had a major effect on my brothers and I in how we deal with relationships. We moved a lot when we were younger; never had a stable home. My mother had a lot of her own personal trauma that she never healed from.

At the age of six years old I was molested by my mother's boyfriend at the time. His name was Gram. He molested me on several occasions. The very first time he touched me, he did it in front of my mother. She had no idea what was going on. I kept that shame with me for a very long time, well into my adult years, until I finally opened up to my mother. She brushed it off as if it didn't matter. Growing up my mother and I never had the greatest relationship, and to this day it's almost as if we're complete strangers. My mother's disregard for my molestation broke my heart. She was the second person I had ever told. Maybe I was expecting something that was not there, but mainly I was expecting her to just be my protector at that very moment. My inner child was speaking to her. The little defenseless girl was crying out for her, but she turned the other way. I felt alone and shameful, kinda how I felt the first time he touched me in front of her. I wear my sexual abuse as a badge of honor now, because I survived a horrific experience, and now I'm able to open up myself and share with others.

My second heartbreak came from my father. I just met him four years ago. He abandoned me early on, and he wanted no part [in raising me]. I decided to reach out to him and find him. It was easy, only took me fifteen minutes. We don't have much of a relationship, because it's too late for him to be the dad I needed him to be twenty plus years ago. My father was the first man who ever broke my heart, and I didn't even know him.

We gotta talk about it. We have to have the conversation about mother wounds. We spend so much time addressing daddy issues and how that impacts us. How it leaves the inner child scarred, but we rarely talk about mother wounds. And let me tell you something, mother wounds cut deep. Some of you aren't ready for that conversation, and some of you may be perpetuating a mother wound on to your own children unintentionally. We are gonna talk about it, so if you're not ready for that conversation yet, skip this section, go seek therapy and come back when you're able to pull up a seat at the table.

Her story is not uncommon. Step into her mom's shoes for just a moment. You are a young mother, doing your best to raise your kids. You don't have a lot of stability because you're moving around from place to place. You're still trying to have a life for yourself and navigate an already difficult world that is oftentimes cruel as fuck. Your child, your daughter, your babygirl is molested right under your nose by someone you trust and you are unaware of it. In addition to this, you're carrying your own unhealed trauma. Only to find that your daughter has been carrying around this deep shame for years. Because you've more than likely endured the same thing, you've numbed yourself to the point of being unable to truly nurture and provide safety for the one person who needed it from you. You couldn't protect her, because you've got no idea what it's like to be protected. So the cycle of mistrust continues. Some mothers don't realize that even when they do the best they can, when they don't address their own personal trauma, it fucks their kids up. What if, instead of blaming our parents we approached it from a place of compassion? What would it be like to come from that place?

Truth be told, you can't give what you don't have. If you don't have the tools, it doesn't work. My own mom and I share a complicated relationship. I found myself having this deep desire to exert my own independence and own my voice, but growing up in a black house with a black mama, you have no voice. This isn't always the case, but growing up in my house it was considered talking back and you're liable to get popped in the mouth for even trying. To this day, I have to choose my words carefully so as not to trigger her. Trauma responses are the norm.

My mom was raised in a house with no love. She didn't hear the words I love you from her own mom often. Her stepfather was verbally and emotionally abusive and she internalized the narrative that she had to be guarded to protect herself from being hurt. When she met my father, he rescued her from that poor situation. He was an escape, but she endured a loveless marriage. He couldn't give what he didn't have. When she tried to step outside of herself and be vulnerable, he didn't reciprocate. So back in the shell she went. On top of his cheating, he didn't show her affection. My mom didn't have the tools, so she wasn't affectionate with her own children. She worked a lot, and was under a lot of stress and, not having the skill set to properly manage her stress and anger, she yelled and lashed out a lot.

You don't realize until later just how much of an impact certain styles of parenting has on you until it's too late. In my case, I learned to shrink. I learned that my voice and having an opinion didn't matter. I learned that I had to perform in order to receive love. I learned that it's better to live my life alone than be with someone who may end up leaving or hurting me anyway. So much so that I made a lot of mistakes (which you'll read about), and repeated the false narrative of unworthiness on a loop. I had built up such a thick layer of armor. Armor so thick that there was a time where I couldn't even feel my own heart. I couldn't feel the beat. I felt so numb. My mom also instilled in us the importance of being independent and not depending on anyone, especially not a man. This manifested in me not being able to reach out and ask for support, creating separation and believing that I had to figure everything out on my own. As I grew, I understood that I can't do it all on my own, nor do I desire to. I wanna lay my head on a man's shoulder and surrender.

Mother wounds cut deep. Whether it's brushing you aside when you tell them you were molested, or telling you you're weak when all you desire is to be loved, to *feel* something, anything. It leaves an imprint. How do we break that cycle? Well for one, get therapy. It helps. Secondly, tell yourself you are worthy every fucking day until you start to believe it. Set boundaries and honor them, even when it feels uncomfortable. Even if it feels like you're disappointing someone. Just as they say when you're a child "one day you'll understand", one day they'll understand. But the days of shrinking yourself are done.

A Practice:

Stand in front of the mirror and look yourself in the eyes. Stand tall like a tree. Feel your feet on the ground. Straighten your back. Let your shoulders relax. No seriously, relax. Your shoulders don't need to be touching your ears right now! Put your feet shoulder length apart, arms down, palms open and breathe in for 4, hold for 7 and release for 8. Repeat. In for 4, hold for 7, and release for 8. Recite the affirmation listed below.

An Affirmation:

I am worthy to be loved.
I am worthy to take up space. I am worthy to open my heart.
I am worthy to let love in.
I will not shrink myself. I will stand tall and accept all parts of who I am.
I am not my mother's choices. I deserve to live a full life.
I choose my life for myself.
I am worthy to be loved.

> *"Be a pineapple: Stand tall, wear a crown and be sweet on the inside."*
> -Katherine Gaskin

Chapter 3

Young and Inexperienced

You think you know, but you actually have no idea.

My Story:

Picture me: A Freshman in high school, 14 years old, weighing in at about 115lbs. Minimal experience in dating. Trying to figure myself out, find my footing, find my voice, and define my purpose. Relatively shy, introverted and reserved. I didn't know shit! My sister had taken me under her wing and I accompanied her to an after school program most days. Who knew that this particular after school program would change me socially, emotionally, and personally. It was there that I discovered my voice, and it was also there that I would have the next few boyfriends throughout my high school years. This one in particular has left an imprint on my life. I didn't realize how toxic we were for one another. I didn't realize how much we were not meant for eachother. But who does at that age?!

Our afterschool program served as a safe space for "at-risk" youth. Pretty much if you grew up in the hood, you were considered at-risk because the hood has its own set of challenges. It just so happened that some of these youth had gone through the juvenile justice system. He was one of them. I remember the day he walked in with his group home mates. I remember thinking to myself,

"Damn, he got some big ass ears...he's cute though!" I remember being introduced to him. I remember the magnetic pull. I remember... Unfortunately, he was 19 (at the time, he lied and told me he was 17..we'll get to that a little later). Legally, we could not be together. Legally, he could go to jail. We didn't care. He protected me with such fierceness.

Since I was not of legal age, I wasn't allowed on the premises of his group home. He'd go AWOL (absent without official leave--basically leaving the premises without permission) just so we could spend time together. It was with him that I experienced the sensation of a first tongue kiss. A first intimate physical touch by a person of the opposite sex (though he and I never engaged in sexual intercourse, some finger action and hickies definitely happened...ugh). A first love. That shit was crazy, Boo! We'd have these fights (mainly arguments) and I'd try to leave but he'd always plead. "No! Ashley. Don't leave me! I love you." I'd push him away or slap his face and he'd run after me. He'd plead for me to stay each time. We were insane and I was foolish. I remember one time we were at the after school program and we had gotten into it over something stupid. I wasn't listening to him and that upset him. He grabbed me by both wrists and had me against the wall. The action was so abrupt and it caught both of us by surprise. He had a look of terror in his eyes, but me...I saw red. I started swinging on him. Blow after blow. "No! Ashley! I'm sorry. Don't leave me. I love you."

At various points in our relationship he'd go missing for periods of time. Sometimes weeks or months. It became a pattern. What became predictable was that every time he disappeared, I knew it was because he had gotten arrested. Once for violating probation. Once for drug possession with intent to sell. Once for vehicular robbery. Once for physical assault. You'd think at my age, I wouldn't be so exposed. I knew way too much! Of course no one approved of our relationship. My mom was not really here for it either. My aunt definitely wasn't especially when she found out "how old he was". My mentors advised against seeing him because he was not stable. Mental health was a thing before I even knew it was a thing. He was a Paranoid Schizophrenic who was also diagnosed with ADHD. I didn't listen to any of the noise of those who disapproved of our relationship because I thought I could change his life. I thought I could be a healer. I thought if he just had some love and stability he would be just fine.

There was never a dull moment. We'd send one another love letters when he'd get incarcerated. He'd attempt to call collect to my landline, but I knew not to accept the calls. Mama wasn't having it AT ALL! Accept a call from where, when you ain't contributing to any bills around the house? Chileeee please! I didn't want the smoke! So our encounters were reduced to him calling and after you heard the automated, "You have a collect call from…" He'd yell quickly, "Hello! It's _____! Tell Ashley I love her! Just tell her I love her"…Automated voice, "Would you like to accept this call?" Haaa! I loved him with a fierceness in my heart though and I couldn't bring myself to end things with him even though it took a toll on me when he'd repeat the cycle of getting in trouble and ending up back in jail. Because remember, I thought I could change his life. There was also the pressure of believing that I owed him loyalty and had to "hold him down" while he was locked up. This went on for a while! Too long.

One time he was out of jail we took a trip on the city bus from my hometown to another city so that I could meet his family. I felt so special and seen. I felt embraced by his loved ones. I felt like I was truly winning. However, that feeling subsided when on the commute back home we were at the very back of the bus. I was laying in his arms and in my opinion he was flirting with a girl in front of my face. She was around his age and I felt a bit inadequate. I wasn't here for the blatant disrespect, so I spoke up. I don't remember what it was that I said to him, but in an effort to hush me, he slapped me. Not hard, but hard enough to embarrass me. Here we go again with this bullshit! I pulled away from him. The thoughts going through my mind at the time were, "Oh, you wanna put your hands on me? It's a wrap! We're fucking done!" Back to the same vicious cycle. "I'm sorry. I didn't mean it. Don't leave me. Ashley, I love you."

His last time being incarcerated was my last straw. I stopped sending him letters. My family and I ended up moving to another part of town for reasons separate from him. It seemed no matter where I went though, he **always** managed to find me. This time, I decided to cut the cord and say, "No more." Damn we were so toxic. Despite the toxicity, he went hard for me. In my 31 years of life, he was the only one to ever buy me flowers. He brought them to my school on Valentine's Day at the risk of being locked up for dating a minor, he was kicked out of the group home for going AWOL, he stole jewelry and gave them to me as gifts, and so much more. I ate it all up, but when you're young, you mistake that attention for love, especially when you had an absentee dad. I know I needed to experience that level of craziness, dysfunction, and madness so that I could be more cautious in the future. I thought I knew love, but I had no idea!

You may be reading this and thinking to yourself, "Ashley! You made a typo when you titled this chapter "Young and Inexperienced", I think you meant young and dumb!" Whatever it was, I simply didn't know any better. At that age, you think you know everything. Let's keep it real, we don't talk enough about predatory behavior. I was 14, dealing with an almost 20 year old who clearly understood laws way better than I did. He knew the consequences he could face if we were caught together. I had a tendency to date guys older than me because they showed me the attention I was craving. There was such an invigorating thrill in being pursued. That's not always a good thing. In that youth program I attended there was a guy there who would always say to me "Yoooo, when you turn 18!!" and he'd look me up and down undressing my then underdeveloped body with his eyes. While he understood the parameters and implications around dealing with a person not of consenting age (and not wanting to go to jail for statutory rape), others choose to ignore that. We have to do better at teaching our youth ways in which to protect themselves. Young girls take that attention and run with it, or they choose to ignore the attention with the hope that by ignoring it, violence won't be inflicted upon them due to a man's bruised ego. I was simply ill-informed at the time and didn't feel safe enough to initiate a conversation with my mom for fear of judgment.

If I could go back in time being the age that I am now, and have a conversation with my 14 year old self, I would hug her and I would say, "You are enough exactly as you are. You don't have to settle just because you fear not being seen. You are whole, complete, and loved. Understand that you can't change people. Change is 100% personal." Sometimes, when you're in it, the best thing you can do is save yourself. Why, though, is it so incredibly difficult for us to save ourselves? Why must we always pour so much energy into trying to change a man? Why is it that we think that if we do all of the right things, that would be our ticket to creating a man who will do right by us, go on a straight and narrow path, and get their shit together? Why is it that we fool ourselves into thinking that love is enough and that as long as we are loved, men can get away with doing the bare minimum? It makes me think about where we actually learn about what it means to be in a romantic partnership. What is your point of reference in regards to healthy relationships? Is it your parents? Is it close relatives? Is it the media? How does that influence the way in which you approach romance and partnership throughout your life? One thing I know for sure, the lessons always come. Some come in the form of hard truths. Some in the form of physical trauma. Some lessons come more subtly and repeat themselves periodically until they're learned.

I definitely had to learn the hard way that until I put my foot down and set boundaries, anyone who entered my life had a free ticket to come and go as they pleased, act a damn fool whenever they wanted to and get away with it. I really had to learn to speak up for myself and not apologize for it. Sometimes we fear that if we speak up, or say how we feel, somehow that would make people run away or distance themselves from us. As if them leaving would be a loss. Like we're afraid of losing a good thing. In actuality, how good could it possibly be if fixed behavior is too much of a challenge? Remember, it is not your job to try and keep anyone. YOU, my dear, are the catch. It is your job to communicate what it is that you need and trust that your partner is going to listen and adjust accordingly. Notice I said adjust, not change. I have to repeat this because for some of you, this went right over your head. YOU CANNOT CHANGE A PERSON. People don't just magically become different overnight. They become more of who they are, and they reveal more of themselves as time goes on. The surprise comes, however, when we fail to truly get to know people before entering relationships. So really take your time. Ask questions. Date. Like *really* go on dates. *Learn* one another. That way you're not ending up in situations where you're literally immersed in dysfunction trying to figure out how the hell you got there. Never feel like you have to succumb to so-called pressures of "loyalty". The number one person that you owe your loyalty to is yourself.

So choose yourself, Babe. On the days where it's most challenging. Choose yourself. On the days where you're at war with yourself trying to figure out why you stayed so long. Choose yourself. When you really want to cave in and accept that apology one last time. Choose you. Because you deserve your love and affection the most. Because you deserve a love that is healthy, stable, and functional. Choose yourself. Because you are so worthy of it. I don't give a damn how much he pleads or says that things will get better. I don't give a damn if there's tears running down his face and he is putting on an Emmy or Oscar worthy performance about how he's going to change and how he's sorry. He's not doing it for you. He's doing it to feed his own ego and you're better than that. You are the catch! You have the final say! You get to create a partnership that *feels* good for you. You get to create the experience that is *in service of you*. Don't allow that man to block your blessing and make you miss out on the opportunity to be with the one who was designed specifically for you. Choose you. Choose you. Choose you. Every goddamn time. Choose you.

A Practice:

Using the space provided, write a letter to your 14 year old self. Knowing what you know now, what lessons would you instill upon her about what it means to love and be loved. What advice would you give her about how to navigate her own love journey? Affirm her. Love her. Embrace her. Give her what your 14 year old self needed during that time. She deserves it.

An Affirmation:

Healthy partnership looks like...

When I am clear about my needs it creates space for...

I will always choose myself first even when...

> *Let change start with you.*
> *The more you learn yourself, the more you'll realize that the choice was always you.*
> *Choose yourself every time.*

Chapter 4

Mind Control

If they feel the need to control you it's because they have lost grip of their own lives

Her Story:

When I met my ex boyfriend he was 26 and I was 21. I was not an "advanced 21" because for the most part my mom was strict, and even when I turned grown I was not grown. So when I met him I was really naïve. He seemed to be a good man. He had a steady, good paying job, a Bachelor of Arts degree, a BMW, and his own place. He also treated me right and made time for me even though he has a kid. I thought I found my king. Somehow it all changed and I found myself begging him to stay with me. He manipulated me into thinking I would never find anyone better than him. He made me forget my worth. He made me feel ugly, and like nobody else wanted me. He made me cut off social media and told me to stay in the house. I did it because I didn't wanna lose my "good man."

The more he saw he could get away with, the more he did. He started putting his hands on me-- punching me, choking me, twisting my arm, putting it behind my back... He told me that as long as he didn't hit me in my face it was not abuse. I stayed for 2 and a half years because he was all I wanted, and in my head it got no better than him. He promised me the world. Said we were going to move in together, have a baby, I was going to meet his family and son. For a long time this is what kept me-- the hope for the future. However, he stopped spending time with me, stopped picking up the phone, and we stopped going out. All this time I had a promise ring. Not to mention, I went out and got his name tattooed on me.

I prayed about it, asked God to help me move on from him, and slowly I was no longer blind to love. **I started to see my worth**, **how beautiful I was**, and how **I deserved love.** Something he was not giving me. We broke up, got back together, broke up, got back together. Until the last time when I said I'm never going back, and I haven't spoken to him since. I was heartbroken because I gave him all of me. Anything he wanted I did. He said, "Jump." I said, "How high?" I loved him with every part of me and it hurt to see I was the only one in love. All I was to him was sex. That's all he needed me for. I was blind for 2 YEARS! **What hurt the most was what I allowed.** Some days I still cry when I think about how I let him manipulate me. But I learned a lot about myself and my self-worth and **I'm healing and growing.**

What you allow will continue. Oftentimes we meet someone and they seem perfect. We give chance after chance after chance because we truly want to believe that there's good in that person. We think, "Maybe if I just change this one thing, or maybe if I just compromise on that, maybe, just maybe...things will get better." They will...temporarily, until that person is back to their old ways and old tricks of lying and manipulating as a means to fuel their own egos and feel superior. A person who feels the need to control you is only doing so because they don't have a grip on their own lives. They have no concept of what it means to stand in their greatness not from a position of authority, but from a place of peace. There's a saying that goes, "If loving someone comes at a price, then it's too expensive." Your inner peace means everything. Just think about it. Have you ever been around someone and when they leave, rather than feel uplifted or empowered, you feel drained? Trust energy. It never leads you astray.

Listen, mind control is a bitch and by no means is true love meant to be compromising. Especially when it comes to your inner being. You shouldn't have to give that up. It's like Aunty Eartha Kitt once said, "A man comes into my life and I have to compromise? You must think about that one again. A man comes into your life and you have to compromise. For what?! For what?! For what?! A relationship is a relationship that has to be earned. Not to compromise for…and I love relationships, I think they're fantastically wonderful. I think they're great. I think there's nothing more beautiful than falling in love. But falling in love for the right reason, falling in love for the right purpose. Falling in love…Falling in love. When you fall in love, what is there to compromise about?" She has such a beautiful point. Love should never be about compromise. The very definition of compromise is to weaken (a reputation or principle) by accepting standards that are lower than is desirable. Keep your standards high. Really define what is acceptable and non-negotiable in your life. You don't have to accept anything that is not worthy of who you are. Your worth is immeasurable.

When I reflect on the queen in the above mentioned story, I'm present to the fact that she understood that despite what she had gone through with that man, she allowed it. We accept the "love" we think we deserve. We ignore the warning signals and red flags that are clearly in our faces. This is not for us to condemn or make ourselves wrong for it, but instead to take these experiences as lessons to help us grow, using our discernment to make better, smarter decisions as we go into the next stages of our love journeys. Understanding and acknowledging that we are so valuable. We are getting stronger everyday. We will not be manipulated or controlled by anyone, especially not any fuckboys who don't have their shits figured out.

A Practice:

We accept the love we feel we deserve. Once you've defined what your boundaries are, it will be easier for you to communicate with your future partner about what lines can be crossed and what things are not up for discussion. Using the space provided, list out your boundaries. On the left, write the things that you want in a partner and on the right, list the non-negotiable boundaries that you will not accept from your partner. An important thing to remember, once you've set those clear, intentional boundaries, be direct about them and don't waiver from it.

What I Want	Non-negotiables

An Affirmation:

When I set clear boundaries, it creates space for...

When I know what I want, it allows me to...

I honor my boundaries by...

Setting boundaries is an act of self-love.

Chapter 5

Pressure Doesn't Always Make Diamonds

Too much pressure can turn out to be shit

My Story:

I ignored a lot of warning signals early on, allowing myself to be led by the flesh rather than by the spirit. I was only 16. What did I know? I was just happy that someone like him--who could have his pick of the litter-- would be interested in someone like me. Don't get me wrong, I had my share of admirers, but my eyes latched on to him. As with most new beginnings, things were fresh, fun and exciting. We would spend time together and talk on the phone all hours of the night. Since he had his license, sometimes he'd take his grandmother's car to come see me and I'd sneak out the house to sit with him and make out. We were just two foolish kids having a grand old time. That is until one day he said, "You know I love you, right?" I was speechless. I thought, "What am I supposed to say? I don't feel this way. I mean, sure, I like him. But LOVE?!" Love was a whole other playing field. One that I was NOT interested in participating in.

I was used to a certain level of emotional intensity. This didn't feel like that. It didn't even feel genuine. It felt like something a guy would say if he was just trying to get in your pants. I wasn't ready for that. I didn't believe him and I didn't feel compelled to say it back. I was becoming increasingly more honest and outspoken but my response caught him off guard. "How can you love me when we've only been together for 2 weeks? How can you be so sure?" To him it must've felt like a real blow to the ego because when I tell you that was THE beginning of the end for us! He became so damn mean. He ignored my calls, stopped coming around, and gave me the cold shoulder when he'd see me. Like, straight up made me feel like shit. He'd say, "I don't say I love you to girls that often. You're fucked up for not saying it back. You don't really care about me." But I did care about him. Just not deeply. His constant gaslighting made me feel bad.

Eventually, I told him I loved him out of obligation. That didn't stop him from being distant. Rather than take that as a sign to just move on, I started participating in shame and negative self-talk. Thoughts permeated my mind like, 'If only I had just said it back when he said it, then he wouldn't be so mad at me. I don't deserve him. If I didn't hurt his feelings, then he wouldn't be ignoring me. I need to explain to him why I had a hard time saying it back initially. I need to go to his house and ask for his forgiveness and apologize.' Do you see where this is going? I got my ass on the city bus and went to his fucking house, Sis! Do you wanna know what happened when I got there? He opened the door, looked at me with this incredulous look as if I'd lost my goddamn mind (which I clearly did) and said, "Did you really just show up at my house unannounced? Are you crazy?" My voice got small, and I replied, "You weren't answering your phone. I feel bad for what happened. I wanted to apologize. I do love you. I want to fight for us." He got quiet for a moment. The silence felt like a lifetime. Finally, he said, "You really want to know how you can earn my forgiveness?" "Yes," I replied. He said, "Okay... I want you to give me head.... & I want you to swallow."

At this point in the text you're probably thinking to yourself 'Bihhhh! Did this muthafucka REALLY come out his mouth and say that shit?! Hold the fuck up! I hope you slapped the taste out of his mouth! Talking about give him head and swallow. Get the fuck outta here!' Literally as I'm typing this, I have the same thoughts my damn self. But yup. He sure did and because I had such *poor self-esteem at the time, I did it. It would be 4 years before I even allowed another dick anywhere near my mouth. It was one of the most degrading experiences of my life. I felt so dirty... so unattractive... so worthless. It happened on the stairwell in the apartment. His grandmother was in the other room. I was so disgusted with myself. Degrading as it may have been, I thought I had "won" because after that day things really started to "look up" for us. He started being the "perfect" boyfriend again. Showing affection, being attentive and communicating consistently.*

As I'm writing this, I can imagine to you this must feel like watching a train wreck in slow motion. Complete and utter destruction. This guy was so not worthy of my greatness. What's even worse, I lost my virginity to him in the bathroom of my old job. There was NOTHING special or romantic about it. I wasn't even in love. It hurt. I felt like I could crawl out of my own skin. I felt so dirty. I honestly didn't even want to do it. But again, the feeling of obligation seeped in. He didn't stick around that many weeks after the fact. I harbored a lot of built up anger and when I'd see him, my body would tense up. Eventually I moved on, but it wouldn't be years until I realized the weight that this experience had on my future relationships and how I chose to show up in the world.

When we downplay our worth to make someone else feel worthy, it only causes us to lose in the end. When we succumb to the pressures to please...the pressure to lift someone else up on a pedestal...the pressure to place others' needs before our own...we cheat ourselves out of the opportunity to truly live. For a while, it seems I stopped living. I asked myself what was the gift that this experience had given me. What I discovered, is that It's given me the courage to stand in my truth. It's given me the courage to say no when I want to say no. It's given me the courage to only do things that I *want* to do. It's given me the courage to not succumb to pressure for fear of being deemed unloveable. To acknowledge that I attract what I am. To acknowledge that respect comes when I respect myself. That can only come when I am truly *in relation-*

ship with Me. When I truly know who I am, I get to define it for myself. When you show honor for who you are and you listen to the voice on the inside that screams no, understand that this voice is guiding you. This voice is divine intervention. Some may call it intuition. Listen to it. It's going to get you out of a lot of tricky situations.

They say pressure makes diamonds, but too much pressure is usually shit. Sometimes we trick ourselves into believing that if we don't yield to pressure, it would scare people away. Quite frankly, if a person is pressuring you, it's because they are dealing with internal societal pressures within themselves. The pressure that comes with growing up. Most boys around my way grew up with absentee fathers or fathers who had gotten locked up. There was a lack of positive male role models to show them the way and teach them how to be men. They were left to figure shit out on their own. In his case, he lived with his grandmother. His point of reference was much different. He didn't have much information to go off of. Not to excuse his behavior in any way, shape or form. I just simply get it now.

As I'm processing this experience, I realize that it was a traumatic one. One that I blocked from my mind until recently. This chapter was harder to write than anticipated because I am now present to the deep impact that it's had on my life and the romantic interactions that followed. For years, I walked around keeping people at a distance. My mindset was that if I kept them at a distance, then they couldn't hurt me. I avoided feelings at all costs. I became very hard inside. Men were disposable. I'd go numb after sexual encounters. I would shut down, close off connection, put my clothes back on and say, "I've got to go." I'd run. Sexual experiences literally made me want to crawl out of my skin. I detached from the experience of pleasure. Numbness became my safety blanket. I couldn't quite put my finger on what the root cause of the numbness was. Pain will do that to you. In a book called "Untethered Soul" by Michael A. Singer, there's a chapter where he talks about pain being the price of freedom. He says, "If you close around the pain and stop it from passing through, it will stay in you." He goes on to say, "If you don't want the pain, why do you close around it and keep it?" I kept that pain in me for so long.

Many of us are walking around carrying the weight of traumatic experiences and it is affecting how we show up in the world. It reveals itself in every aspect of our lives. It impacts our social interactions and what we become triggered by. It even influences the types of roles we take on at work. It literally interferes with the ability to form meaningful soul level connections. What if we just allowed the pain to be what it was, accept that it played a role in our lives, but not allow ourselves to be victimized by it? What if we didn't give it power to hold significant weight in our lives? What if we simply let it go? I know it's easier said than done, but that's the beauty of doing the *heart* work. We're always going to have to heal from something, so why not start with letting go? By holding on to the pain and giving it so much energy, we block freedom. Don't you want to be free? Don't you want to know what it's like to feel and have that energy reciprocated? Don't you want to know what it feels like to be safe? To feel at home? To allow your soul to rest at ease knowing that all is well? Release that pain, Babe. It's time.

A Practice:

When we're in the thick of it, oftentimes we don't realize that we're partaking in a traumatic experience. We don't realize the weight or impact that it has on our mental health until we break free of it. Sometimes that can come weeks later. Sometimes it takes years when we've evolved and leaned into a deeper sense of self. Some will call it a spiritual awakening. Some will just call it discernment. Either way, when it reveals itself, you'll know. In the space below, journal about a romantic [or not so romantic] experience in your life that greatly impacted you. What did that experience teach you? How are you better in spite of it?

An Affirmation:

Inhale through your nose. Exhale out and meditate on these words:
My soul rests easy knowing that it didn't break me. I'm still here, so that means I matter. I'm supposed to be here. Look at me, thriving. Surviving. Living and learning. Yearning and earning everything that was meant for me.

I'm a warrior.

> *"I'm a survivor. I'm not gon' give up. I'm not gon' stop. I'm gonna work harder. I'm a survivor. I'm gonna make it.*
> *I will survive and keep on surviving."*
> *-Destiny's Child*

Chapter 6

Situationships

"Situations will arise in our lives but you gotta be smart about it."
-Usher

Her Story (QP):

I was in a relationship with a man for 4 years and not once did he refer to me as his girlfriend. After all was said and done I was forced to reconcile with the fact that I broke my own heart, and he played a significant role in the performance.

In the beginning he would wine and dine me (dinners, movies, birthday gifts, and parties). We were together every day for at least 3 weeks. I was sleeping over his house, I met a couple of his family members...we were a thing--or so I thought. I ended up asking him many times throughout our relationship what our title was, and every time he'd avoid answering the question directly. He would remind me that he thinks he'll end up being alone for the rest of his life.

Eventually, over the course of our relationship I fell out of love; however, I still loved (and still love) him. I started to pay more attention to the red flags like not being invited to family functions and not being introduced to ALL of his friends. In fact, I found out one of his friends that he considers his best friend didn't even know I existed. That was the final straw for me.

Even after attempting to move on I found myself back in the same place with him. Thinking this time we would just make it about sex. However, there are still feelings coming from both parties. I had to decide [for myself] to stop giving in to the foolery.

You deserve to know where you stand in a man's life. If you're dealing with someone for a length of time and things are getting serious, it is your right to know where things are going. You may feel like you are in a relationship, only to find that the other person only sees you as someone to spend time and vibe with. Vibes do not emit exclusivity. Vibes do not emit a title. Vibes are just that…vibes. Now let me not be mistaken, vibes can be a great thing if that's what you're personally looking for. However, if you have the intention of building with a particular person, it's only right that you find out if you guys are heading in the same direction, or if you need to abandon ship and go your own way. The sooner the better, because when reality sets in that you've been playing yourself and the relationship was actually a situationship, it's a sucky space to be in. It is absolutely essential that you be completely honest with yourself.

Fuck a grey area! Get clarity. *If a man wants you and is serious about building with you, you won't have to question it because he will be **clear** in his **intentions** and his **actions** will be in **alignment**.* Re-read that sentence and really, *really* let it sink in. Highlight it, write it on a sticky note, save it in your phone. Do whatever you have to do to keep it present in the forefront of your mind. Nine times out of ten we usually know where we stand, but we try to convince ourselves that we're being delusional, or that we're trippin and being insecure. We make ourselves wrong for wanting to know. We apologize for asking for what we need. We shrink. Our voice gets small when we utter the words, "So what are we?" in anticipation for the answer we already know. When we get the answer, we try to bargain with ourselves. Thinking maybe he's just not ready at this moment. Let me just give him a little more time. Let me show him how valuable I am and why I would make a good girlfriend for him. Let me just do this or do that. Babygirl! Stop. You are entering compromise territory. Remember, **love is never about compromise**. You considering those thoughts is a clear warning signal on the inside telling you to run. I was watching a segment of The Steve Harvey Show called "Ask Steve" and one of the things he said to a woman who was going through a similar situation is, "Don't get in the habit of collecting red flags. *Don't* collect red flags. You're gonna have a wagon full of em. You only need one." Pay attention to those warning signals. The moment you spot **one**, that's *all* you need. We have a tendency to want to wait things out or see how things play out. It's not necessary.

As you can see in the queen's story, they tried things out, stopped talking for a period of time, and then reconnected again thinking maybe they could just try sex, before her finally saying enough is enough. It's all a cycle. Get off the hamster wheel! It **never** leads to commitment. A man who wants to commit will commit. If he doesn't see your value, you do yourself a disservice of trying to convince him to see it. He won't. Here's the thing… ***you will never be enough for the person who is not meant to be in your life.*** Stop trying to make the puzzle pieces fit. It's a completely different puzzle. Your puzzle is magnificent and his is basic as fuck, Sis! It is in no way, shape or form nearly as great as what you've got going on. Leave him to figure his shit out *on his own*. He's a grown ass man and you are not responsible for him. Point. Blank. Period!

One more thing, soul ties are a real thing! It's what happens when you give your body to someone and the emotional or spiritual connection still lingers long after you have stopped dealing with that person. Rather than suffer from a sexually transmitted disease, you instead suffer from a spiritually transmitted disease. Some people think that they can just casually sleep with whoever they choose and don't believe that it would have any type of effect on their beings. This ideal is false. Anytime you have sex with someone (whether it be vaginal, anal or oral), there is a physical, emotional and spiritual exchange that occurs. For women, we tend to bear the brunt of the effects because there is an outside entity (a penis, if you will) that is entering our bodies. The effect is even greater if the act is performed with no barrier. Make no mistake though, it doesn't have to just be between a man and a woman. Soul ties aren't sex or gender specific. It can happen to anyone. Don't fool yourself into thinking that you can just be with someone sexually and have it have no type of effect on you. Your body is literally a temple. I am not trying to parent you. You can parent yourself. Protect your heart and spirit, being mindful that an exchange is happening. Energy is energy. Be intentional about who you allow into your space and as always, take care of yourself.

A Practice:

Red flags take on many forms, shapes and sizes. Be clear in what you want to look out for, and when you spot it, get the hell out of dodge! Simply put, you are way too valuable to waste a second more of your time with things that do not serve you or lead to a dead end path. Using the space provided, list out the red flags that you may have ignored in the past that ended up biting you in the ass. This way, if it comes up again, you'll know to keep it pushing so that the cycle doesn't continue.

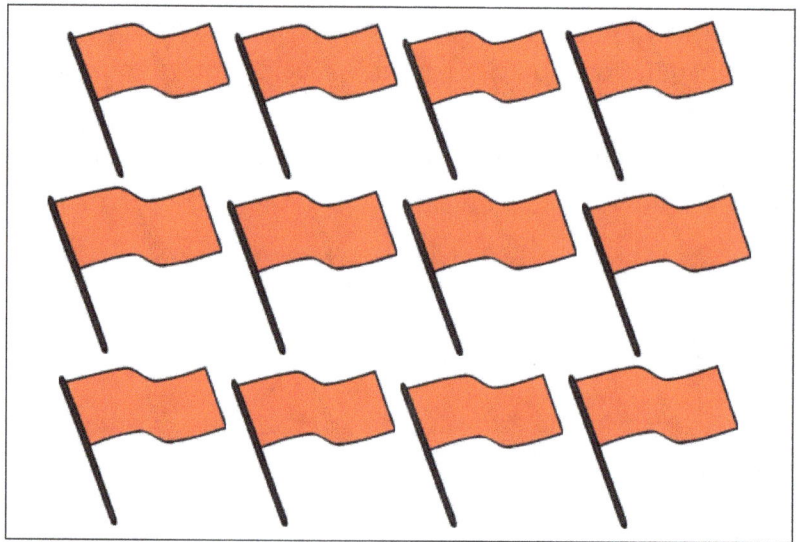

An Affirmation:

Sis, repeat after me: I am love. I am power. I am beauty. I am brilliance. I am raw. I am real. I am unapologetically me. I deserve everything that I desire. I am worthy of commitment. I am worthy of true love. I am worthy of peace and pure joy. Uncertainty is a red flag I can't afford to take a chance on.

> *"Don't commit to me. Commit to evolving...I'll meet you there."*

Chapter 7

Hurt People, Hurt People

You can try and make others feel the pain that you feel, but really you're hurting yourself

My Story:

Dear Lover,

Over the course of our relationship everything I tried to do was centered toward pleasing you. I tried to play the role of the supportive girlfriend. I tried to be loving, compassionate and understanding. I accepted you as you were and tried to help you sort through the baggage you carried so well. I tried to help bring some order and stability into your life. I believed that everyone deserves to be loved and share that love with someone else. In order to prove my love for you was real, I was very affectionate. I told you, "I have so much love to give." Being that you had been "hurt", it made it difficult for you to accept the love I had to give you. It was something you weren't used to and so you rejected me repeatedly. Each time this happened, I took it personally. It made me feel like there was something wrong with me. I felt like I would never be good enough for you. Later, I learned that you felt I was doing too much. So it made me feel like if you didn't want my love, then what did you want? Sex? Friendship? I was lost and confused. I was hurt.

I felt like I was giving 80% of myself and you were only giving me 20% of you. I couldn't understand it. While I was doing so much to prove my worth and get you to open up, you had built emotional connections with two women online, going as far as meeting and spending the night with one of them. I felt defeated. How could the man I care so deeply for drive out of his way to another state and sleep over at a woman's place that he only knew from the internet and play house with her and her daughter? I made that mean that you didn't value me. So I sought companionship elsewhere. I saw my ex at a party and met up with him afterwards. I didn't tell you the whole truth. As far as you know, we only kissed, but we actually had sex. Honestly, it was a cry for help. A cry to be heard, validated, understood. I felt so alone in our relationship. Though I acknowledge that what I did was wrong and I hurt you in the process, reflecting on this experience has given me a newfound perspective on the events leading up to the infidelity. My subconscious reminded me of what was lacking between you and I. Real love. When I love, I love hard. When I'm with someone, I'm all in. I didn't feel like it was reciprocated.

We all have our truths, but here's mine. Throughout the course of our relationship, I cried countless times. I cried when you flirted with other women. I cried when you allowed women to call me out my name and disrespect me. I cried when you gave out your number to people (including one of my friends) when I asked you not to. I cried when you allowed women to call you "hun, babe, sweetie, boo, baby, etc..." I cried when you made me feel ugly for getting a haircut. I never felt like you stood up for me when I needed you to, except that one time at work. I felt a sense of unworthiness knowing that there were pictures of your ex in both your phone and your laptop that you told me you were going to delete. I felt like a sidechick knowing that I received an exact replica of the gifts your ex received for Valentine's Day. So many times I've tried talking to you and voicing my concerns but I just didn't feel heard. Automatically, there would be an assumption that I was trying to argue, get an attitude, or I'd be labeled jealous, insecure, and accused of acting like an ass. This letter isn't to put you down or make you seem like a bad person, because I am far from perfect. I reacted a lot. Far too much. I didn't always seek to understand.

Honestly, there was just a level of maturity that we both were too young to fully acquire at the time. If we're to be completely transparent with ourselves, we weren't ready. As much as we thought we were. We weren't ready to be in a relationship and part of me feels like you felt tricked into being in one with me. The emotional security was lacking and we both ended up hurting each other. I physically cheated, and you emotionally cheated. It doesn't make it right, but it's the facts. I was really angry after we broke up, but you breaking up with me was the best decision you could've made. Only then could the real work begin. We weren't perfect, and we tried the friends with benefits thing afterwards. I admit, that my suggesting it was a form of trying to maintain control. However, when we really let go, things looked up. We learned ourselves and ultimately we grew. I know you were hurt and upset with me for awhile after learning that I had gotten pregnant by someone else and undergoing an abortion, but I had to do what was best for me. The decision wasn't easy, but it had to happen. Thank you for loving me through it. Despite all that we went through, I have no regrets. I have no ill feelings toward you. We cared for one another once upon a time. I wish you the best in all of your future endeavors. I wish growth, love and vulnerability for you. May you be what you could not be for me, to a woman who is deserving of it all. But most importantly, may you heal first.

With Love,

Ashley

This was the letter I never had the guts to send. Seems putting it in a book was in a way therapeutic. But there are a few layers to unpack here. You cannot fully commit to a relationship if you have not done the **heart**work on yourself to heal. ESPECIALLY if you're coming out of a long term committed relationship. In my case, my previous relationship was one in which I thought I'd be with that person forever. In his case, he was engaged to his ex and it didn't work out. That's some heavy shit. We didn't give ourselves time to unpack that baggage. Instead we carried it into the next situation thinking it was going to unpack itself. In addition, we didn't provide ourselves with the loving care we needed FROM ourselves after giving everything and receiving no return on investments. It's no wonder that he was emotionally unavailable. What people do to us is not personal. I need you to understand this. Their behavior is not excusable and all must take accountability for their actions. However, the act in and of itself is not personal. They are only doing to you, what has been done to them. It is not your job to heal anyone. Leave that shit to the professionals! You do yourself a disservice by taking on someone else's load when you haven't even dissected the pain and trauma you have experienced.

Fill your own cup first. Be your own healer. Sometimes we find ourselves in these rebound situations because we want to feel loved. We want that human connection. We crave intimacy. But at what cost? The cost of being in a whole relationship with someone that you barely even know, trying to wing it as you go along. Someone's bound to get hurt. There's a certain level of emotional maturity that is necessary before you begin any relationship whether it's a friendship, romantic relationship or business partnership. You must show up grounded, clear, complete and open. You must understand conflict resolution, communication and partnership. You can't go in projecting your fears and insecurities expecting that the partnership is going to be long lasting. It's not. You're setting yourself up for failure. More than anything, the ability to be dependent on yourself to give yourself what you need is crucial. Some of us don't take the time to adequately heal and learn ourselves before we jump into new relationships. Then we end up building bonds based on codependency. We want to feel needed, loved, desired, wanted, but go about it the wrong way.

You've got so much ahead of you. You're not running out of time. You're exactly where you're supposed to be. The person meant for you will show up when you're ready to receive them. Do the heartwork.

Don't skip any steps. Allow yourself to **be** with heartbreak. The healing process is supposed to be ugly and messy. Go through it anyway. That's the only way you're going to grow. Don't be another hurt person projecting your hurt on to others. You'll lose in the end and that's just not how you're built.

A Practice:

Sis, I chose him rather than choosing myself. Every time you decide to stick with a situation that you know is not healthy or fulfilling your needs, you are not choosing yourself. Many of us are choosing hurt over self-love. In the space below, take some time to reflect on these questions: What would it take to treat yourself as your ideal lover? Do you even have an idea in your mind of what your ideal lover looks like? What would it take to gain the clarity and understanding that you deserve?

An Affirmation:
I will fill my cup first before I choose to fill someone else's.
My happiness matters.
I will put myself first every time.
I listen to the voice on the inside. She's protecting me.

When I heal myself, I heal the world.

Chapter 8

In Denial

One hell of a drug

Her Story:

It was my Senior year of college. He was tall with an athletic build, his skin the color of dark coffee with two swigs of cream, and he wore cornrows going straight back. Every Monday, Wednesday, and Friday after class I would see him in the main building amongst the football players. They all seemed to be looking up to speak to him as if they were all needing his approval and competing for his attention. I stood in the main hallway of that building greeting my girlfriends; them having random discussions, me half way listening and looking at him look at me. He gave me that look that said he was intrigued, but for several weeks we would dance this dance.

A few weeks later on a sunny day he walked up to me, extended his hand and introduced himself outside of the cafeteria. I found out that we were from the same city and I knew his brother, who was really close with my sister. The formal introduction was memorable. I had heard all the lame college dudes pick up lines and attention seeking actions, so he really stood out to me. We exchanged numbers and the rest was history.

History... My history now includes heartbreak, single motherhood, and 4 years of child custody hearings...

Red flags were there from the beginning. Most importantly, intuitive signs. I would wrestle with myself to just stay in the relationship that was toxic and going nowhere fast. A couple of females came out of the woodwork. I would confront him and by the time he finished his manipulation and lies, I was the one apologizing. (Sad, I know) I forced myself to believe him. He would threaten to break up with me and would say I was insecure. I became a person who would trash houses and confront women. I would tell myself the incidents of other women were subtle hints, and when I get "black and white" evidence that he wouldn't be able to deny, then I will walk away. He even went as far as giving me his password to his phone to make me feel comfortable enough to not snoop in it, which was further manipulation. Until that one unfaithful night...

I stopped talking to my family and friends about our problems because I knew what they would say. I failed to mention the fact that he spent four years in prison sharpening his manipulation skills. I didn't see him being an ex-felon as a red flag because of the fact that he was in school bettering himself. Later I realized that college was a cover up, and he had been involved in criminal activity while we were together. He would change his number often and two years into my profession (his senior year) he was arrested in a highly publicized case in which they named him the ring leader. Yet, I stayed and he told me he was innocent. I begged for my family to help and when they would ask hard questions about the case I would become defensive. Off the strength of me (despite the trepidation) my mother paid the retainer for his top notch criminal lawyer. For eight months, he was in jail until his family decided to leverage their home for his bail. He was sending me fourteen page love letters. I would visit him in jail (the search, degrading) and we would talk through a nasty, clouded, written plexiglass. I was down in every sense of the word, literally down. I later found out "love" letters went out to many different girls during that 8-month stint.

Fast-forward, he was bailed out and while he was still fighting the case I became pregnant with my first son. A beautiful brown boy who immediately became the love of my life. The hold his father had on me, this twisted, dark, manipulative, volatile bond didn't seem so strong anymore. When I was 3 months pregnant, I was cleaning his old boy's room while he was away. A call came through his iPhone. It was his mother calling for me on his phone. "Darn it, I missed the call. Let me call her right back." I proceeded to put in his password and returned her call. We spoke for a few minutes. Then I hung up, put the phone down, and while it was still unlocked, a message from "Brian" came up. The message was very "suspect " in a gay way. I decided to call the number and found out Brian was really Bianca. After years of not snooping through his phone because he gave me his password, I became Detective Gadget! I looked through numbers, texts, pictures, and videos. I found out that Michael was really Michelle and the "friends" who were married, he was actually sleeping with. I also decoded the "bro code" he, his brothers and closest friends had. They were having orgies with random girls in local hotels and yet I was oblivious. There were even conversations about illegal activity on the phone. So much information and I was given the password out of manipulation to not look. I was 3 months pregnant and devastated...

The Black and white evidence I needed was right in my face. It was menacing and down right cruel how the words from each text stared and glared at me. I had my evidence and as far I knew, this relationship was over.

That Friday night I became a single parent. I left and never looked back. Although I was courageous to leave, that pain was serious and debilitating at times. I couldn't drink or party the pain away, I couldn't date it away, and I couldn't sleep it away. I had to go through it sober and pregnant. Although we weren't married, I still had to divorce, kill, and bury the possibilities of being a happy family. I had to grieve the discontinued plans and dreams. **I also had to forgive myself for not advocating for or loving myself, and for ignoring my God given gift and power-- my intuition.**

Leaving had its consequences but it brought me, Me. I know my strength and worth. When it came to love, I got out of my own way. I didn't date the first two years of my son's life, but I now have a man who loves me and it feels *so good. He even loves my child like his own.* **I showed him how to love me after I learned how to love myself.**

"I showed him how to love me after I learned how to love myself." How many of us are out here trying to learn how to love ourselves? & because we don't really know ourselves or know the proper way that we want to be loved, we are settling for less than we deserve? How does one even begin the process of learning that? Where do we even begin? How many of us are suffering in silence for fear of judgment or being told the very thing that we don't want to hear? How many of us are ignoring our intuition because we want to convince ourselves that we just need more proof? I've been there and let me tell you, in denial is one a hell of a drug. One that will leave you staying in dead end relationships way longer than need be, acquiring way more than you bargained for. Only to be left feeling empty and depleted because you gave all you had inside and starved the one person who needed you the most...YOU.

You need your love. You need your affection. You need your time. You need your energy. You need your compassion. You need your attention. You need your honesty. You need your loyalty. You need YOU to fight for you. You need YOU to build you up. You need YOU to grow and become the best version of yourself. You can't do that if you've emptied everything you have inside of you and poured it into something that you knew was toxic. Some of you are reading this and it's triggering. It should be. I'm not writing this to make you comfortable. You picked up this book because you wanted more for yourself. You picked up this book because you're tired. You picked it up because you wanted someone to give it to you straight, in service of your growth. I told you, I'm coming from a place of love. You deserve it.

I once related to love as a struggle. I felt like we had to struggle or go through some shit to make our love stronger. While loving partnerships have their share of ups and downs, that is not synonymous with putting up with bullshit or staying longer than need be, hoping for things to change or get better. It doesn't mean that you have to fight yourself everyday to stay when everything inside of you says go. Love is actually synonymous with ease, grace and passion. Listen, you deserve sooooo much. Do not be afraid to give it to yourself because as you can see, when this Queen made the conscious decision to walk away, it provided her with the opportunity to lean into self-love and be open to allowing the right one to treat her the way she deserved to be treated.

So, you have to start over? Big fucking deal. Starting over is so damn promising! You learn so much about yourself in the process. It's never too late. You might be 60 years old. Guess what, there's a woman out there that just turned 75, met her king and is living her best life. You better have some faith and honor that you deserve more. You ARE more. & don't you dare for another second allow anyone to manipulate you into feeling any less. This woman said that this guy was in the wrong and by the end of it, SHE ended up apologizing. Don't let that be you. If you identify with it, it's time to clean up shop. I love you, Girl and I'm telling you, if it threatens your peace, leaves you up at night worrying and anxious, or makes you feel unworthy, it ain't worth it. Remember, your inner peace means everything. Trust yourself to be okay. Trust yourself to get back on your feet. Trust yourself to handle your business, ESPECIALLY if you've got a young one watching you. You teach your babies what it means to keep it pushing. You teach your babies self-love and self-acceptance. You teach them real power. It's all you. So let's go, you badass, fucking powerhouse, you! Self-love is waiting on the other side, Babe.

A Practice: Let that mutha fucka burn!

Using the space provided, list the mindsets, beliefs or ways of being that you're choosing to set ablaze because they no longer serve you? What were you once made to believe was true about you, that you now know are false? What was projected onto you? Let it burn.

Gaslighting: psychological manipulation of a person usually over an extended period of time that causes the victim to question the validity of their own thoughts, perception of reality, or memories and typically leads to confusion, loss of confidence and self-esteem, uncertainty of one's emotional or mental stability, and a dependency on the perpetrator (www.merriam-webster.com)

I set this mindset ablaze...

I set this way of being ablaze... (ex. needy, desperate, helpless, victim, etc)

I once was made to believe...

I know this is not true, I am...

An Affirmation:
I release what's not meant for me and embrace change so that I can open myself up to all possibilities.

> *Walking boldly in my truth that I am a badass capable of anything I desire.*

Chapter 9

Strangers

Do you even know who you are?

My Story:

"Stranger"

Verse 1: How could you even step to me and think that we would still be cool? How could you even step to me and think I'd wanna talk to you. With all the games you played, the words you said and all the things you did? I don't think so. You've got to go. We are not friends. Just don't say nothing.

Hook: Treat me like a stranger. I mean nothing to you. Treat me like a stranger. Go do what you wanna do. You don't know me, from Adam or Eve. So treat me like a stranger. Stranger, stranger, stranger.

Verse 2: Oh, the nerve of you to sit by me and look me right in my face. Ooh if people weren't around I'd slap the smile right off your face. You give me a bad taste. Never thought I'd have so much hate. Remember when you said I was dumb as hell? Had no morals? Not who you thought I was? & how you told me to kill a part of me?... Scared that I'd ruin your life... as if you were living right.

Hook: Treat me like a stranger. I mean nothing to you. Treat me like a stranger.

Go do what you wanna do. You don't know me, from Adam or Eve. So treat me like a stranger. Stranger, stranger, stranger.

Bridge: & if I never see your face again, that would be just fine. I won't mind. Treat me like a stranger... treat me like a stranger... Walk on by.

Hook: Treat me like a stranger. I mean nothing to you. Treat me like a stranger. Go do what you wanna do. You don't know me, from Adam or Eve. So treat me like a stranger. Stranger, stranger, stranger.

"Stranger" © 2011 Ashley Burney All Rights Reserved

He watched me for weeks. I was a college student and I transferred from Uconn's large Storrs campus to their smaller regional campus. I took an hour bus ride to get to school and another hour bus ride to get back home. I wasn't thinking of no damn man! In my mind, men were distractions. My main priority was getting this degree. I had already faced dismissal from the university before, and this was my chance to not fuck it up. I had to stay focused. I felt him staring at me. He was very attractive. Tall, athletic, but not the bulky kind. His stare, intense. Though I tried to avoid eye contact, I was drawn to him. We made eye contact briefly and I looked away. It was kinda my shy girl way of flirting. Before you know it, he approached me. I don't even remember exactly what he said, but as it turned out, he had been watching me for a while. Conversation just seemed to flow. He was a beautiful stranger. We exchanged numbers. From there we talked everyday. I was weary of hanging out with him initially because I was just trying to get my education. But he...just had a way with words. I felt comfortable. So our first hangout was at his place. We met at the local Dunkin Donuts for a tea, and walked to his apartment. Since he didn't live too far from my school, we agreed that I would come hang out with him before going back home.

When we arrived, we talked for a bit. I learned that he was a soccer player. He was originally from Jamaica and he has a cousin who lived in my area, so he traveled to my city quite often. I didn't even intend on having sex with him *that day. I wanted to maintain my good girl image and not give up the goods on the first meet up. One moment I'm getting up to leave his place. The next moment, he's taking my clothes off, bending me over and fucking me from behind. "I knew you wanted me to do that. You kept saying you don't have sex with guys you don't know that well, but you secretly wanted me to do it." Did I? Perhaps a small part of me had that inkling, but verbal consent was not given. I didn't have that option. It was taken away from me. Since I was the relationship girl after all, I felt like maybe this was a push for me to loosen up. Maybe it wouldn't be so bad to just have no strings attached sex. In my mind I didn't stop him, so I guess it was okay. Perhaps I did actually want it.*

Fast forward, we're fucking on a regular now. Meet up. Hang out. Converse. Fuck. Repeat. We go to his spot. We go to his cousin's house and chill in the basement. We pretend to watch movies. Fuck. This went on for quite some time. Meet up. Hang out. Converse. Fuck. Repeat. Then one day, I started to feel strange. What's happening to me? All of a sudden my senses are heightened. Certain smells just seem to get to me. My appetite started changing. No… This isn't happening to me. Ha! Surely not me. I still have school. I have to complete my degree. Nausea. Peeing on a stick. Plus sign. No! No! No! I tell my sister. I sob. I curl into the tightest ball on the floor of my mom's room and bawl. My world is a blur. Disappointment. Panic. Fear. Horror. This can't be happening to me. I'm not ready. I'm only 20. Fuck. I have to tell him. I have to tell my mom. I don't want to. Can't escape it. You made your bed…now lay in it.…Fuck!

I call him. I tell him, "I'm pregnant. But don't worry, I'm not having it." Then the doctor's appointment confirms what I already know to be true. They scheduled me for an ultrasound two weeks out. I go reluctantly and now I hear a heartbeat. I see the monitor. Thump, thump. Thump, thump. Thump, thump. Thump, thump. I'm having second thoughts. My mom is disappointed. We made the abortion appointment and she doesn't want my life to be over. She's so disappointed she can't even be in the same house as me. Tears fall down her face as she heads for the door, grabbing her keys, slamming the door, getting in her car and driving off. I wanted to die. I felt like I had no one to turn to. Seems the only people remotely excited at the prospect are my sisters. I reached out to a mentor of mine and she was able to help me put things into perspective, but I still felt so alone. Knowing that I would have to pick up the phone and call this man and tell him I'm having second thoughts. I called him. This time updating him on the ultrasound appointment. I tell him how I'm not so sure anymore. The switch up was like the flick of a light turning on and off. This charming guy ain't so much the charmer anymore.

"You're dumb as fuck!" He screamed. "I can't have a baby. No, no get rid of it! I'm going back to Jamaica to live. You have no morals! You're not who I thought you were. I don't fucking know you! You can't have this baby. I won't be around. Kill that shit!"

Shame. Hurt. Tears. Disappointment. Self-loathing. Even worse, Chlamydia. So not only am I pregnant. I contracted an STD from him. Negative self-talk. Depression. Suicidal thoughts. Die, die, die. Why me? How could I be so stupid? Why didn't I make him wear a condom? What did you think was going to happen, stupid? Everything he said about you was the truth.

I endured the procedure with mom and my sister nearby as a support system. But the Depression around that time was real. The deep sadness. The tears. The silence. The pain hurt worse than anything I could've ever imagined. I don't regret the decision to have an abortion. It was a decision that I had to make for me. I knew that I wasn't ready. How could I even be anyone's mom? How could support a child mentally or financially? It just wouldn't have been the best decision. I deleted his number and blocked him. It wouldn't be almost a year before we ran into one another and he apologized for the way he behaved. For the things that he said. For not being there through the process. I forgave him, but he ended up trying to sexually violate me a month later and I cut the ties completely.

I ended up facing dismissal from the university yet again due to being unfocused and off track. All that money could have gone down the drain because I was running behind a dirty dick fuckboy with a weak pull out game. Focus on your goals, girl. I could've lost everything. Not saying that a baby ruins things. It's our own individual choices that dictate the direction in which our lives go in. I knew that I couldn't bring a baby into this chaos. Not for nothing, I allowed him to violate me more than one time. First with the initial sexual encounter. Then, there was the demeaning words and tone in which he spoke to me when I informed him that I was considering keeping the baby. Finally, when he almost sexually violated me again.

When we fail to communicate clearly how we desire to be treated, it becomes a whole field day. Guess who's the one being run all up and down? Yes. You. So speak up. Your life matters more than anything. Your goals matter. Channel your focus on something that will yield the best return on your investment. It's so easy to get caught up in the heat of the moment when you're being showered with affection and attention, but will that person stick around when the going gets tough? Will that person stick around when the outcomes are less than desirable? Will they still treat you with common decency and respect even when they don't agree with your decisions?

This guy said a lot of fucked up shit to me, but he was right about one thing. He *didn't* fucking know me. We didn't know each other. We hadn't even been dealing with each other for that long. Maybe two months at best and I became pregnant within those two months. Take your time. Get to know people. Let them learn who you are. That way you don't have to spend a lifetime explaining yourself and what you desire for your life. Prioritize friendship. At the heart of every relationship, you must have friendship. If you're going to be engaging in casual sex, make his ass wear a condom. I don't give a damn that it feels better without one. If you know you're not looking to have a baby anytime soon, you need to protect yourself. After that moment, I now ask so many questions. Men literally have to earn the right to explore my body because it's my sacred space. I wanna know the facts. I wanna know if you have any diseases. I wanna know if you have kids. What the dynamics are of the co-parenting partnership if you do have kids. I need to know everything. Life is way too short and in my situation, it could've been so much worse. What if I contracted a viral infection by being careless with my body? This would be a whole different story. I said it before, and I'll say it again. PROTECT YOURSELF. It's the only thing that matters. That and your mental health because once you lose that, that's it.

A Practice: Reflect on this question. What is something that you haven't forgiven yourself for? What would it be like to experience complete and total forgiveness of self? If you've already forgiven yourself, who is someone in your life that you haven't forgiven? Write them a letter. Don't send it, the letter is for you.

An Affirmation:

My body is...

I show honor for my body by...

I take care of my mental health by...

> *My body belongs to me. My pussy. My rules.*

Chapter 10

See the Signs

Trust your divine intuition

Her Story:

"I'll see you later"

He had said this to me around 3pm, on a Friday afternoon, right after he had told me of his evening plans that would involve catching up with his friend from his term abroad in Germany. Of course, being the trusting girlfriend I was, I had assumed he meant it. Little did I know it would be 3am, and I would be the one up all night crying until my head throbbed like the bass in a BPM song.

She lived below me, directly below me. As in, her apartment was literally the one directly below mine and if I wore heels, she knew. She and I had been friends since my freshman year, bonding over a mutual adoration for opera and Ralph Lauren. She and he had met whilst abroad, and him being the dark brooding handsome type that he is, she had feelings for him and would deny it to anyone who asked. But I knew. I always knew. And being the friend I was, I had asked her if it was alright if I dated him when he had asked me.

They went to Germany with ten other students from our college, and came back with stories to last a lifetime. Drinking beer in this abbey here, and spending loud nights at a disco here...I enjoyed hearing the stories, but not once did she admit her true feelings, the true story underneath the veneer of glamourous German life.

That night, they planned to watch a movie and catch up, as they hadn't seen each other much, given that he and I had been spending every minute together. So, there they are, a floor below me, and there I am, a floor above them. I'm relaxing and drinking a glass of wine, watching something meaningless on Netflix, just biding time while I wait for him to come upstairs and see me. He had promised he wouldn't be too late. But he was. He was hours late. Texts were left without responses, calls were ignored, and I even gathered the courage to go downstairs and press my ear to the door. When I heard nothing I went upstairs and tried not to assume the worst.

Days later, I would learn my assumptions were correct.

She told me in person, he was too much a coward to face me, and called me over winter break.
How could he? How could she?! It was such a deep betrayal, I didn't want to face it or my feelings wholeheartedly. I couldn't help but blame myself. If I had been a few pounds heavier, spoken in cute voices, or had a snarkier sense of humor like she had...maybe then he would want me. It had to be that. We had been so solid for five months, I must have done something wrong, or something must have been wrong with me. That's what it was.

A week later, I forgave them both, a mistake I would soon come to regret deeply.

A few months later, there was a planned German 'reunion' of sorts for the students and staff who had been on the trip. They were a close-knit group, it was nothing out of the ordinary. The months leading up to that night had been strange. He and I hadn't been intimate, he blamed his guilty conscience for that. Said he couldn't do things with me for fear of hurting me, or seeing her. That was a dull pain compared to the knife that was sinking deeper and *deeper into my back. Unbeknownst to me, they had been talking to each other, confessing emotions and desires that I always knew they had, but they would never admit to anyone. Three words were exchanged time and time again, and yet, there I was, standing by my man like a fool.*

The night of the Germany reunion arrived, and again, I was upstairs, occupied this time with one of my roommates. Auditions for a musical were in the morning, and we were taking an easy night, watching the movie version of the show, jokingly preparing to cast it ourselves. Their whole group had come back early, and had enjoyed their time together, and he had texted me they were hanging out in her room, the girls were getting ready to go out.

And that's the last I heard from him. The next time I would see him would be at 4:47am, strolling into my bedroom.

This is where it gets interesting.

This is where whatever existed between them had gone and died.

She had always been proud of her high tolerance, her ability to outdrink anyone by at least four beers. She proclaimed her 'tank' qualities at every pregame, every party, always. However, this time, she claimed she had had too much and didn't remember anything past the dinner. But she miraculously regained consciousness when my boyfriend was between her legs. Funny.

He claimed she had come onto him, and he couldn't control himself. She had this hold over him, that he couldn't explain, and I didn't understand. I still don't. But at least I felt he was always honest.

She then proceeded to claim he had assaulted her, and he claimed she was lying. I did not know who to believe. She was friends with my friends, and he was friends with my other friends…either way I was put into a difficult situation. Yet, not one person was asking about me. Here I was, broken again, betrayed again, and no one was asking about how I felt, or what I needed, or what I was going to do. I have never felt so alone.

Losing my first love and a best friend for good. I couldn't forgive them after this. I didn't care to listen to her nonsense story about drinking too much and not knowing what she was doing. She was desperately trying to absolve herself from feeling any guilt, but I was the only one who could see it.

To this day, I'm the only one who saw it.

I was afraid, lonely, and easily manipulated into taking him back. This time, for a lesser position. Now, we weren't even a couple, we were in this strange place of 'friends' who would sleep together every night. He had what he wanted: me, and the freedom to do what he wanted with whomever he wanted. I thought I had what I wanted, but watching him shove his tongue down another girl's throat at a party a few weeks later solidified my decision to end things, once and for all.

He still didn't see a problem with anything he had done to me. Even though I had finally seen him for the pig he was, I still felt that something was wrong with me. What had I done to drive this man to do this? What was wrong with me? How could this have happened to me, not once, not twice, but essentially three times? To make matters worse, I still loved him, I still wanted to love him, the man I thought he was, at least. I questioned what love even was at that point, and if I even knew what it was. How could it exist when I had given everything I had to a man who was so willing to use me and toss me aside? How worthless was I, really? I spent two years wallowing in my pool of low self-worth, covering it up beneath layers of makeup, false smiles, and loud laughs, hiding the truth from everyone. No one could love me, because the one person I had chosen to, thought I wasn't good enough. I had completely given up.

But there was a small part of me that still wanted to fight. I still craved love, I wanted to be loved and I realized that what I had with him, wasn't love. And I realized I deserved it. I found my light again, and was slowly becoming myself again, the vivacious, sparkling, and exuberant woman I always was, but couldn't see. When I realized that this was never love, I felt freed. I wasn't stuck within this fixed definition that had let me down. I knew that when I *really, truly, found love, I'd know that I'd be grateful for this lesson. And that all the pain would have been worthwhile.*

And it has been.

Ladies. We are the most powerful beings in the world. We possess within us an inner power that no other species on this Earth has. We have something called Intuition. Though every human being has intuition, nothing compares to that of a woman's. A woman's intuition is so strong that it has the power to literally move mountains. It has the power to heal. It has the power to provide so much clarity and insight. If you feel something in your gut, you know that it's the truth being revealed. What tends to happen, however, is that first it comes first as a slight nudge. So we ignore it. We think, 'Oh I'm just tripping. It's nothing.' Then that nudge becomes a slight tap. We think, 'Oh, you're being paranoid. It's nothing. Shrug it off.' Then that tap becomes a slap. We say, 'Hey, something might be a little off, but nah. I'm just tripping. Shake it off. Shake it off." Then that slap becomes a whole body slam and we're like "damn! How did I not see the signs? How could this happen to me?" You've been getting signs all along, Babe. But instead you tried to assume the best or give people the benefit of the doubt. But really, who ends up with the deception? Who ends up with the pain? You.

The queen in this story saw the signs very early on. She knew that her friend had feelings for her guy before she even started dating him. She wanted to believe that nothing would happen. She wanted to believe that it would all be fine. She wanted to believe that the feeling or inkling would pass. But what happened? Those feelings developed over time right under her nose exactly one floor below her. Trust your intuition ladies. It's a gift. It will save you so much heartache and pain if you choose to empower it. Your body is always giving you signals. The universe is designed to work *for* you, not against you. Pay attention. Heed the warnings.

Growing up I had this story that women couldn't be trusted. "Don't bring your friends around your man," my mom would say. "You never know if they want what you have. Keep your relationship private. Nobody needs to know your business." I mean, who could even blame her for saying it? My grandfather cheated on my grandmother with her best friend. So I was conditioned to believe that women were competition. I carried with me a strong desire to protect what I had at all costs. But here's the thing about that, if it can be easily taken away, it wasn't yours to begin with. We've all heard the saying, "What's for me won't miss me." This context definitely resonates within this queen's story. She trusted him and he lied. She trusted her and she lied. She wanted so deeply to believe that neither of them would deceive her, but something was missing. The thing that was missing was the trust in herself. The trust in herself to believe that she deserved more. That she was worthy on her own. That she could stand firm and say enough is enough. The reason why her so-called friend could even get close enough to her guy is because he hadn't given his full commitment. She allowed him chance after chance with no real accountability.

What's beautiful about this story, however, is we get to see the metamorphosis of a girl into a grown ass woman who not only changed the narrative and took back her power, but wrote a new story that enabled her to finally live in her truth. The truth that this guy and girl were not worthy of her greatness. That she could generate a healthy relationship that is rich in love, trust and honesty. One that is solid, safe and FULL. One where she doesn't have to wonder where he is, what he's doing, or if he's being truthful. No, this new relationship is 100% in service of her. When I asked her what qualities her new beau brings out of her, here is what she had to say,

> "[He] makes me feel so so loved and so appreciated. With little things, as small as a kiss on the head or a little whispered "I love you" as we fall asleep, he really shows me how much he cares for me. He and I

have built a strong relationship, definitely based on trust and appreciation. He and I frequently tell eachother how much we appreciate the little things the other does. [He] encourages me to push myself and get out of my comfort zone both personally and professionally and because I trust him, I know everything he says comes from a place of love. Even when we fight it's usually over something small, and then we make eachother laugh and apologize and it's over. He really brings out the silly and sweet side of me, and after [the other guy], I used to hide it because it made me vulnerable and I didn't want to really open myself up and get hurt again, but he loves the silly side of me that no one really gets to see. He has helped me work through my self-esteem issues, my trust issues, and my vulnerability. He has always wanted to hear my secrets and my embarrassing and crazy stories, and to get to know the real me. He loves all my flaws, my insecurities, and helped me realize my strengths lie within my weaknesses. But most of all he's shown me what love really is, and I'm so thankful for him."

Breathe that in, Sis. Ponder her words. Revel in it...because that can be you. Real love is liberating. Real love is honest. Real love is healing. Real love is transparent. Real love is vulnerable. Real love is raw. Real love is possible. Sometimes we try to hold on to people, not realizing that the very people we're trying to hold on to are standing in the way and blocking you from your life partner. There's so much power in letting go. So much power in allowing yourself the opportunity to truly be seen for the goddess that you are. So much power in allowing the one whom God/the Universe/Spirit specifically designed for you to enter your world and give you all your heart desires and so much more. Open yourself up. Let that toxic person go. Your husband is waiting.

A Practice: Self-trust is everything, Sis. Sometimes we stay too long knowing we should leave because deep down we don't believe that something better is out there. We don't trust ourselves to be worthy enough for healthy, fulfilling, rich love. But we are so worthy and we have to start listening to the subtle warnings on the inside. They're here for you. Using the space provided, journal about a time where you ignored your intuition and it cost you in the long run. Journal about another time where you followed your intuition and it saved you a lot of unnecessary trouble. What did those experiences teach you?

An Affirmation:
Divine intuition is a message straight from the ancestors.
I'm listening.

My soul rests easy knowing that I am protected at all costs.

Chapter 11

Get Your Life

Narcissism is a Muthafucka

***My Story:** *Name in this story changed for confidentiality purposes**

"Hold on... May I help you?" He holds his hand up in a surrender-like way as if to convey that he's harmless, "I was driving by and I saw you standing here. Are you okay? ...Do you need a ride?" I mean...given the fact that it's 2am and I'm standing alone, I could see why he might be concerned, but I say with a smile, "I don't know you, I'm not getting in your car... What's your name anyway?" He tells me his name and I repeat it. "Olusola? What kind of name is that?!" "I'm from Nigeria," he says. Mind you... my friend is on hold and I'm still waiting for my booty call to pick me up! I say, "Well nice to meet you Olusola from Nigeria. I'm Ashley. My ride is on the way. Maybe we can meet up for tea or coffee and talk about your weird name. Do you have a card?" He smirks, taken aback by my boldness. "A card? No I don't have a card," he replies. "Well take mine," I say. We exchange a few more words and he walks away. I realized then, that my best friend is still on hold and I proceed to put my phone back up to my ear at the same time that my fuck buddy is pulling up. My best friend is cracking up on the other end. "Girl! You crazy! Who was that?" I tell her I have to go b/c my ride is here and that I'll fill her in later.

That was the start of our on again-off again friendship. This 6'4" venti, caramel machiatto of a Nigerian invaded my space in several ways both for good and for bad. We met up the next day at one of my favorite spots and had lunch. I learned that he's an Engineer and he's super driven. He seemed to have a good head on his shoulders. Very smart, goal oriented, in school to further his education. I sized him up. Our bond grew over time but I felt like I was giving so much. I never truly felt empowered around him or felt like things were equal between the two of us. I always felt like he had a sense of superiority despite the fact that I too, had a lot going for myself. I was in college. I had my own health business. I was making my own money working with the youth, and I had begun the process of changing career pathways. Needless to say, things felt odd and I felt pretty torn. Torn because on the one hand, he was someone who was very sure of himself, but on the other hand he had values that clashed with my own. He seemed to have this incognizant belief that women were designed specifically for men's pleasure. I always had to be the one performing oral (willfully, because I enjoy it), he never let me cum first before releasing himself after mere minutes, and to top it all off, he'd never performed oral on a woman, let alone fingered her to make her feel pleasure.

Despite this, I appreciated our friendship. We were able to laugh and joke with one another and talk about anything under the sun. I deeply appreciated the richness of our discussions and that he was genuinely interested in what I had going on in my life. But in the midst of this friendship, I learned that he actually had a girlfriend. So all that time we were hanging out, engaging in sexual activities, he was going back to his girlfriend like nothing happened. I felt like the wool was pulled over my eyes. Though he was honest with me about it, I still felt a way because I wished he'd been upfront in the beginning. Throughout our friendship we periodically had this on again, off again dance with me being the initiator of the distance because I felt like I wasn't always valued as a human being. Despite his many attempts to humanize me, it still left me in a disempowered state. I fought hard to set boundaries because I didn't want to be viewed as a homewrecker. But those boundaries were crossed multiple times. Each time a boundary was crossed I pulled back. Our friendship was very codependent and if I'm to be completely honest, he danced on the err of narcissism. Now I'm not tryna say he's a narcissist or anything, because I'm not qualified to diagnose anyone, but he definitely had some questionable qualities.

Everything was about him. His pleasure. His thoughts. His comfort. He had a way of making you feel like you had to cater to or tend to his needs because he was so nice to you. I just hate that we vibed so hard only to find that he was leading this whole other life. Simply put, it wasn't working for me. When I made the decision to end our friendship, I felt bad. I got sucked back into his world and to me, that was dangerous because he was a wild card. The tipping point for me was when he got married and eventually had a baby, but was still making references to missing my lips. He'd say some weird shit that was really off putting. Things like "wear a dress" or "wear that lipstick I like." Or he'd call me at odd hours expecting me to be readily willing to throw clothes on and come outside to see him. Then he'd try and guilt trip me by saying things like "I just needed someone to talk to" or "you just cut me off". Somewhere in this, I truly believe I did the right thing in creating distance because underneath that nice, gentle exterior is a man on the verge of exploding...& I wanted no parts of it.

Imagine... You meet someone and they seem great. Great conversation. Great head on their shoulders. Great job. Well put together. Great sense of humor. You vibe. They seem grounded and you think, "This might be my person. The search is over. We finna be on some happily ever after shit!" Then they hit you with the "I have a girlfriend" schpiel. **Bitchhhh! The fuck you mean?!** Shit like that would have you ready to give up on relationships altogether. Like **you mean to tell me, this seemingly handpicked guy ain't my guy? Make it make sense.** But believe it or not, this story is not uncommon. Don't let it take you make you bitter. Every so often, he would reach out just to see if I am still accessible to him. For the most part I choose not to answer.

You don't owe anyone your time. Especially if they have a whole wife and kid. As a matter of fact, don't even make the mistake I made of entertaining the thought of a friendship. You're going to be the one looking like Boo Boo the Fool while he builds his family. All because you're trying to maintain a friendship that's not even worthy of your time, energy or commitment. Run, Sis! Get the hell out of the way and save yourself! The last thing you need is anyone ringing your phone trying to come to you as a woman. You know how it goes. The guy does the dirt and his lady approaches YOU like you're the one with the obligation to her. You've got too much ahead of you. Let him watch you walk away. Walk in your purpose. Your blessings are being manifested. Believe it or not, someone out there is manifesting you. Praying for you. Hoping for you. Searching for you. He's not going to find you if you're caught up with someone else's trash ass man.

One other thing to note, this guy was a trash ass lover anyway. ***The fuck you mean you never went down on a woman? Grow up.*** You're designed for a grown ass man, Sis. One who has no problem engaging in fellatio and prioritizing YOUR pleasure because the mere thought of pleasing you brings him to climax. He's on the way, girl. Keep doing the heartwork. It makes a difference even when you feel like you're going to be single forever. Keep going. Keep pushing. Keep setting boundaries. Keep honoring your worth. You fucking badass.

A Practice: If you spot it, run Bih!

Narcissistic Personality Disorder

```
T Y U L M X B R I L L I A N C E
N P E Y B E N T I T L E D C A E
E A C T C S U Y J L M N O T C I
D R N I N S I A Q B N N A N Q U
I E E L G A H E E T C W A Y B X
F H C A C A R A U E A G Q V C K
N T S N R G U C I B O P U N B D
O O E O O T T T I R G U T E X I
C H L S Y M E Y R S M V O N U S
L C O R H D Y A W J S Q W S M O
M Y D E V I T A L U P I N A M R
X S A P Z U P O W E R T S M N D
R P H G R M S F N Y X F R T X E
C H I L D H O O D D Z Y N C I R
Q I X I P H B A W D E F T Q G C
X K H W Y A C M O A K A H Y U N
```

ADOLESCENCE
ARROGANCE
BEAUTY
BRILLIANCE
CHILDHOOD

CONCEITED
CONFIDENT
DISORDER
ENTITLED
ENVY

MANIPULATIVE
NARCISSISTIC
PERSONALITY
POWER
PSYCHOTHERAPY

An Affirmation:

When I spot the signs, I will get the hell out of dodge.
I'm too fucking magical to not be treated like magic

"Boy I made up my mind. This is the end of the line. This is the end for me and you. Boy I'm telling you we're through. I'm leaving you."
-Ashley Burney

Chapter 12

Toxic Masculinity

"Fuckboy" is Non-Binary

Her Story:

My particular situation speaks to what men are allowed to do, and it also alludes to toxic masculinity, the system of patriarchy, and who performs these institutions in our personal lives. I add this note, as my story is in reference to a masculine identified woman, who was significantly more manipulative and toxic to me than any relationship I have been in, including those with men. This is not to say the problem here is queerness, as I have had amazing relationships with women after this, but this added a further element of confusion and betrayal.

This relationship started as casual sex, after a night out in this small city. I have worked with on campaigns with this person, looked up to her, and had been acquainted with her before we were involved sexually. She was older than me and we moved in similar spaces, making everything that much more messy. We also lived around the block from one another, making our connection even more rapid and toxic.

I'm not sure it even started off fun. However, in the beginning I felt incredibly seen. It was pivotal to be with someone even more "out" than me, as up to this point, I had only dated women who were still not out to their families.

I was in love with the idea of this woman and who I got to watch her pretend to be in various spaces. I pretended to be ok with her coming and going as she pleased even after finding out there was someone else she was calling her girlfriend the whole time. I was kept at a distance, but she expected all of the intimacy and commitment from me without showing commitment TO me. I always think of begging her to not sleep in my bed after we had sex, as it confused me. Yet, every night she would find a way back in. Like a lot of other spaces.

The same performance I watched her create in spaces was now performed in my bedroom, as she used feminist and liberation theory to justify her behavior. She would also demonize me for attempting to engage in this same behavior. It was increasingly hard to watch someone who I respected as a scholar use this same theory to manipulate my emotions and actions.

I fell out of contact with my close friends, who became angry at my changed priorities, and frustrated with me returning to someone I denounced and swore to be done with time and time again. I began rapidly losing weight. I became overwhelmed with worry and embarrassment. She found a way to appear in every aspect of my life, but also continued to give me an escape from the job and school I hated. All the time, I knew about this other woman she continued to be in a "relationship" with and present in ways she would not allow herself to be with me. All the while, she was also checking my phone, checking my life, checking me and questioning my queerness and loyalty. I know it was wrong. I know she was with someone else. I know I made those decisions. With that said, manipulation is a hell of a skill.

I became so far outside of myself. Engaging in drugs and drinking, disconnecting from more and more people. Continuing to believe the shit she fed me. I also mimicked this toxicity, all in the name of "love." I don't write this to say I was victimized in any sense, as the toxicity in me definitely rose to the occasion. I attempted to stop this situation multiple times, blocking and deleting her on everything, staying away from her, telling people I was done, all of it. I communicated my boundaries and I tried to have this end. I'm not sure

I tried hard enough. I continued trying to make decisions I could be proud of, and trying to be the "bigger person," while silently suffocating. This dynamic came to a messy catalyst (that does not need to be detailed here) and I continued to go back.

My breaking point was seeing her come the furthest out of character when the threat of losing her girlfriend was made clear. That was it for me. Finally I saw that I was not the person she loved or cared for. Rather I was an escape for her from her responsibilities. My heart also broke for the other woman who continued to be embarrassed by her actions. I'm positive she has found someone else to terrorize, while stepping outside on her girlfriend.

I changed my number and still have her blocked on everything. I stopped going out and navigating spaces she would be in. I engaged in meditation, church, sobriety, and creation to attempt forgiveness. With that said, the fake Instagram pages and emails I receive to this day still vibrate a feeling of dread through my body. As well as a feeling of disrespect I am unable to put into words.

I would not wish that level of torment and harassment on anyone. I would not wish watching people who claim to love you, side with someone they have also watched kill you from the inside out. I would not wish to have to purge your entire life only to find yourself under the layers of shit someone else has made you think you are. I would not wish to be disconnected from reality because of someone else's gaslighting. I would not wish to be another person who fell for someone else's behavior, and then find out you are far from the only one. I would not wish this experience on anyone...including her.

The biggest realization from this entire situation was how we heal. This is going to sound like an Instagram realization but really. That shit takes time and that shit takes effort and that's some shit I will never give to anyone else for any price. I saw her in everything and everyone in these attempts to heal through spirituality and forgiveness.

Until I began exercising. While we were together, I began feeling anxiety physically, in my stomach. This was the one thing I could not shake, until I started physically working her out of me. There is a lightness I have felt in the last month that I cannot put into words, until I have started exercising the places in my body where I have found trauma has been stored.

This shit is not about her. It was never about her. I have accepted who she is, what she is navigating, and what she has done to me and women before me. And I am ok with it. We see what we want and who we want. I realize that nobody lies to you to "protect" you. I realize what brokenness feels like, and I realize the true journey that healing is. I think forgiveness comes later. I know I forgive myself and truly that's enough at this point.

The most terrifying realization has been the amount of times I am met with "yea that's the same shit that happened to me," when I share this story with other femmes. Sending love and healing to anyone who has been through toxicity and heartbreak. Peace and love.

This is like a textbook definition of a toxic relationship. I like to believe that it falls under 4 umbrellas: communication, control, emotional sensitivity and sabotage. Let's start with communication. In a toxic relationship, there's no room to partner when one is not able to reach common ground and be open to hearing the other party's concerns and make adjustments accordingly. Sometimes they become angry, deflect or gaslight.

Which brings us to control or manipulation. This may not always be the case, but in the case of this queen, her partner was older. Sometimes what can happen when we date significantly older partners is that they subconsciously take on a more parental role. In a sense, they're able to easily manipulate the situation because they understand that we may be driven to please, especially if our relationships with our own parents were estranged. However, it doesn't always have to be the case that the party is older in order to become a toxic relationship. When we feel like our partner has a "my way or the way" complex, the partnership aspect goes out the window. One of the worst things that I've encountered when it comes to romantic partnerships is manipulation. They will literally have you thinking that you're bugging or you're crazy. It's not the case. What you're feeling is valid and in most cases, it's spot on. Trust that shit.

Emotional sensitivity comes in the form of you feeling like you have to walk on eggshells because you don't want to set a person off or make them upset. Since the person that this queen was dealing with was so well-known and respected in the community, I'm sure you can imagine the conflicted feelings of how to properly end things without it backfiring on her. Many times we try to consider other people's feelings and the impact that us stepping away will have on them. It's a power leak, Babe. Do what needs to be done for your own sanity. When the sabotage comes and you're made to be the bad guy, it's not pretty. There's a saying that goes, you're the villain in someone's story. Be okay with being the villain if it means you have your peace.

You deserve to be with someone who is not going to leave you up at night wondering if you're worthy. You deserve to be with someone who is healthy. You deserve to be with someone who is not going to manipulate you to the point where you lose your sense of self. You fucking matter. Anybody who can blatantly disrespect you, expect you to not move on from them and make you feel like they're the best you can ever get is not worth your time. Easier said than done, but imagine how you're going to feel when you finally break free. Break away, Babe.

A Practice:

On the eggshells, write what you know to be true about yourself. Who are you at your core? When you're done, take a hard look at it. Understanding that walking on eggshells causes you to lose a sense of self. So much so, that you become barely recognizable. Stay true to who you are.

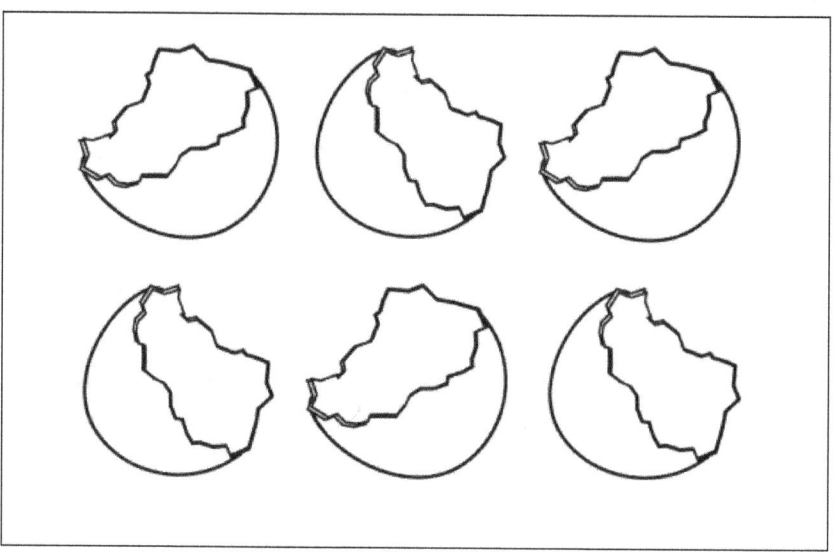

An Affirmation: (Fill in the blank space)

My love is too

_____

to have thrown back on my face.

(Inspired by "For Colored Girls Who Have Considered Suicide / When the Rainbow Is Enuf by Ntozake Shange)

"You need to stay out of my way." -Jhene Aiko

Chapter 13

Fear

Love Should Make You Feel Safe

My Story:

"*Toxic*"

Verse 1: Dealing with you is like drinking poison and we all know the outcome of that. You're a beautiful perpetrator disguised as a beautiful angel. Well, I know better. You're the devil. When I look into your eyes it feels like you're looking through my soul. All of a sudden I grow cold-old. Frozen over. Then I get colder. I'm stuck in space. Lost in a trance. Can't break from your embrace.

Hook: Ooh baby you're toxic. Ooh baby you're toxic. I said baby you're toxic. Toxic for my life.

Verse 2: And I hate you because I can't escape you. You're everywhere I turn. When will I ever learn-earn-earn? You're bad news! You got me breaking all the rules of the things I said I wouldn't do. I got to get away from you.

Hook: Ooh baby you're toxic. Ooh baby you're toxic. I said baby you're toxic. Toxic for my life. Toxic for my life. Toxic for my li-i-i-i-ife.

© 2012 Ashley Burney All Rights Reserved

He had eyes so damn intense. Those piercing eyes, that physique, that height, those lips. E-Ver-Ything in my body tingled in more ways than one. His whole persona screamed of danger, but there was also a sweet tranquility about him. We hadn't spoken a word to one another; only made eye contact from a distance. I was out with my oldest sister and her friends sitting at the bar area, and he celebrated a friend's birthday with others in the same venue. When we were leaving I saw him outside eating cake. I mustered up enough liquid courage to ask, "Where's mine?" Without hesitation, he cut a piece of the cake with his fork and fed it to me. Stop playing, bitch. I was HOOKED. His quiet power, feeding me and that sexy little smirk that danced on the corner of his lips was all it took to have my nose wide open. I knew that this would be the very guy to take me out of my comfort zone and introduce me to some things I'd never done before.

My sister, her girls and I lingered outside of the bar laughing and talking for a bit, engaging him in friendly conversation and banter. We learned that he was a Boxer and had been to jail before. He was recently released, so in honor of his newfound freedom he decided to go out and have a good time. My sister and her friends mingled with others and I stood with my back facing him, trying to play it cool. Inside, I was nervous as shit. His presence was thrilling and intimidating. As my back was facing him, I felt the slow, sensual, calculating touch of his big, strong hands slowly slide down the length of my little ass, and expertly navigate his way directly to my panties. He slid my panties to the side and finger fucked me from behind. It was clear from his skill and expertise that this wasn't his first rodeo. The fact that he was much older than me gave me a whole other thrill. And whew chile the chills that were sent down my spine! I could melt right there on the spot...and melt, I did. I tried to act normal, but I have it that at least one of my sister's friends knew what was up. You may [or may not] be thinking to yourself, 'Oh issa whole heaux phase!' Well, I was young, fired up and I welcomed it. We exchanged contact information, my body still pulsating from the after effects of climaxing all over his fingers. We agreed to meet up later, but I panicked. When I got home, that rushed feeling of danger within me was heavy. I was intrigued, but so damn cautious; so I passed on the opportunity to get my back blown out that night. As weeks went on, I pushed that warning signal aside. Up until that night, I'd played things so safely. He'd be a new adventure for me to explore...and he was. The next few months would be a whirlwind.

We spent a lot of time talking on the phone and texting. His texts didn't always make sense, but he was fine as hell, so I rolled with it. He would come by late at night and we'd sit in his car and talk. We didn't have sex right away. I appreciated that he respected my boundaries in the beginning. I felt like I was his woman. When we'd hug, he'd pull me into him, kissing me sensually. I felt safe, yet also completely immersed in the wild. He would pleasure me by hand and we'd make out. I felt like I would eventually give up the drawls, but I decided to take my time. I was always scared to go there with him because he was so strong. I wasn't even a virgin at the time, but he made me feel so inexperienced.

The day I finally agreed to go to his house, we entered a dark apartment. I sat on the couch in the living room. He went into the bedroom for a moment. I heard rummaging around before he finally emerged, taking me by the hand, leading me inside. I laid next to him on the bed, and he gently pulled me into him. We began making out.
"You want me?" he whispered in my ear.

"I don't feel comfortable having sex with someone who's not my boyfriend."

He paused for a split moment before replying, "Do you want to be my girl?" I knew he was just asking so that he could get in my pants, but I was kind of afraid of him. So I said, "Yes."

He was now on top of me, kissing me sensually. Before I knew it, my panties were off, his dick was out and he was putting on a condom and entering me. He was huge! His broad chest, those shoulders and that heavenly scent was delectable. While the sex was great and it was the first time I experienced an *orgasm by penetration, I couldn't help but feel uneasy inside afterward. Not to mention after we had sex, his pops showed up. He's an older man so I couldn't understand why his pops was there. I thought, "Is this really his pops' home, and not his? What's the deal?" Forgetting the fact that this man had recently gotten out of jail when I met him. I didn't question it at the time. I felt special just off of the strength that I was being introduced to one of his parents.*

As the days went on, we would talk on the phone. Whenever he did come by to pick me up he'd always have a police radar playing low from his phone listening in. He'd drive up the street to a dark area, and we would have sex in his car. I always felt like I didn't have a choice. If I lied and said I was on my period, he'd say "take the tampon out, I'll put my jacket under you." I was afraid to say no to him. His physique alone was intimidating and the fact that he was in a profession that certified his hands as a lethal weapon. I didn't want to take any chances. I was also a tad bit dickmatized because I was literally having orgasms everytime we had sex. Him being so gentle in how he spoke to me, yet also speaking more sternly when needed established a certain level of trust. I knew he could hurt me but I trusted him not to. I did what he told me to.

I found myself wanting more from him. More time and more attention. His busy schedule didn't necessarily leave a whole lot of room for me. He never took me out on dates. He didn't mind seeing me in the daytime, but I just wanted to be acknowledged. To know that this was more than sex. To know that I was thought of. Then, I didn't hear from him for almost a month. I couldn't understand it. How could he look me in my eyes, kill me with that little smirk, hold me so close to his heart, make me orgasm over and over, then fade away into the background? I was hurt, but I picked up my bruised ego and decided to move on. Then one day I unexpectedly received a postcard in the mail. He had gotten arrested. I thought "Aw hell, not again. We are not holding an inmate down any more. Been there, done that. I'm good!"

Honestly, I dodged a bullet. Years later when he was released, I discovered that he was seeing another woman and he would literally beat her ass on the regular. I don't know why God spared me from ever experiencing that, but I do know that I am eternally grateful. It wouldn't be another few years before an encounter outside after hours with another individual would cause his life to be ended by a bullet. May his soul forever rest in peace.

What I desired was to feel a sense of safety and security. I thought I was getting that safety and security since he was close to my oldest sister's age, comfortable in his masculine energy and fearless in his assertiveness. However, I mistook his mischievous ways for mystery. This man was leading a whole other life. A life of crime and passion. This grande white chocolate mocha of a man with an extra shot of espresso made me melt and freeze at the same damn time. He was a literal mindfuck. Just being in his presence made me shrink. I didn't think that I could stand in my own power. I didn't think I could say no to him, because in my mind there was this intrinsic fear of retaliation. My body was sending out warning signals screaming "Danger!" but I ignored them thinking they were just butterflies. I thought I was supposed to be a little anxious around a person I liked. The person that is meant for you will feel like ease, grace, safety, and peace **not** anxiety.

Being with him showed me exactly what I desired…to feel safe. Up until that point, my relationships hadn't made me feel safe. I remember when in high school I was dating a guy, and on our walk to his house some blocks away we were approached by two men. They pretended to have knives on them and attempted to rob us. What were they gonna get? No fucking idea because I was broke as fuck! So anyway, I was prepared to fight, having had a knife of my own in my pocket. In my mind, "You might try to take me down, but I'm going to leave you bruised and battered as well." While I had a look of fearlessness in my eyes (more pissed that this was happening), my boyfriend at the time had a look of terror. We were saved by the sound of an ambulance siren, which turned off as quickly as it sounded its alarm, almost as if to signal to the perpetrators that they were being watched. That situation made me create a narrative that men were weak. I believed that men were supposed to be protectors and my boyfriend was afraid to protect me. So I treated him as if he were a weak coward.

Another incident happened where I met a couple of friends at a bar and there was a guy there who wouldn't leave me alone. He was harassing me, and I noticed two men standing close by watching. I elicited support from them, but they just laughed at me and shook their heads. This incident caused me to create a narrative that men don't protect women, nor hold one another accountable when they make other women feel unsafe. This narrative drove how I experienced men. So when I met *him*, with that strong athletic stature, I thought finally...someone who I can rely on to stand up for me should I need it. However, that feeling of being on edge never went away. That feeling that danger was lurking in the distance remained because he was always on edge listening to the police radar. His anxiety made me feel like I needed to be looking over my shoulder.

This need to feel safe in a partner and in my own body has shown up numerous times throughout my life. Whenever I thought I was safe, something would happen to reaffirm the story that I needed to protect myself at all costs. Living life in survival mode is exhausting as fuck. ***I, you, we*** all deserve to be in loving, compassionate, committed, wholesome, safe, grounding relationships that feel like home. Relationships that feel like a breath of fresh air where you can lay your burdens down and just...*be*.

A Practice:

Using the space provided, journal, draw or doodle about what it means to be in a loving and safe relationship.

An Affirmation:
I am Safe.
I am Loved.
I am Home.

When I heal myself, I heal the world.

The Tipping Point

These next few stories are all mine to tell. These lessons are ones I've had to learn the complete hard way. I had to fall flat on my ass and face the hard truth that I had played a significant role in the patterns that kept repeating themselves. It was only when I got tired of my own bullshit and realized that I was the person I'd been searching for, that things finally began to open up for me. These next few chapters are all about healing and real growth. Truly, truly stepping into the heartwork, getting messy and facing my shit head on.
Get ready.
Strap in.
It's about to get rocky!

Chapter 14

Taking Back the Key

"I can't wait to hate you, make you pain like I do. Still can't shake you off."
-Mariah Carey

My Story:

Am I selfish? I wonder…am I selfish for hoping you'd choose me? Am I selfish for hoping that it's over between you two? Am I selfish for wanting to push my own agenda and views? Views that if it were meant to be, you would've never initiated a separation in the first place? Am I selfish? Am I really selfish for wanting to make you wrong and me right? For wanting to put up a fight. For caring too much and speaking too little. For thinking of my own needs and desires. I mean…is it really wrong to want you to want me the way that I want you? I mean…am I selfish? For being angry…and confused…and distrustful…of you because like a thief in the night you pursued me and watched me carefully for 2 years before I let you in…Like a thief in the night you lured me in and made me care for you. Like a thief in the night you stole a piece of me, but now it's starting to feel more empty like a void wanting to be filled, waiting…anxiously. Am I selfish? Am I selfish? For thinking of withholding the very thing that draws you in? For thinking of withholding all that is inside of me for the sake of my own protection and security. Am I selfish? Am I really selfish to think that if I just fall back, you can make a choice. A smart choice. The right choice. Is there even really a right choice when you still love her? In love? I don't know, but either way there's something that is making you stay…I mean…love prevails, right? Love wins…everytime. That's what they always say. But in this case I'm having a little trouble accepting it. I'm having trouble because while I'm a mirror of possibility for everyone else, you became a mirror of possibility for me to see that I can let my guard down…not too much though. A mirror of possibility for me to see that…I could be someone's wife someday…just not yours though. You've already got that part covered. A mirror of possibility for me to see that I can have someone…someone who looks at me like art. Like I am a masterpiece. A gem. A mirror of possibility for me to see that I could have fun, and be messy, and vulnerable…not too much though. Pull back, dry your eyes, he doesn't like that, chin up, buttercup…you knew what it was before you chose to make that step. To go that route. It's not your place to pick a fight because you're not together anyway….deep breath. Inhale. Exhale. Relax…. You said I scare you. You said I scare you. I scare you because you're falling for me. & I never intended for you to fall at all. Actually, I never intended for me to fall… You said when you see me, you just want to be around me. Not even on a sexual level, but just to hold me. Because this connection we have is so strong and that's something you look for…connection. You said WE need to figure this out because you can't do it alone, and I can't do it alone…but we must. & if by chance we end up together great. If not, I have to accept that because I was never okay with being second best. I release you…I release you…I release you, graciously. I release you…despite how much it's pulling on my heart strings. I release you…because as hard as it is, it's the right thing to do. Deep breath. Inhale…Exhale…Dry your eyes. Chin up, Buttercup…Relax.

I tried to do it…Lord knows I tried to do it..but I can't. Or maybe there's something in my brain that's preventing me from being able to shut it all off completely. My thoughts, feelings, body sensations…they all seem to point in the direction of you. & that's the most confusing part about all of this, because it seems the harder I try to run, the more I am being pulled into you. It's like a drug. Seems like I'm just waiting on my next fix. Gotta have it. Just a little taste though. Too much of anything isn't good for you, right? But damn I just can't seem to figure out why it's so hard to get you out of my thoughts. I'm in a trance. Lost in space. Distance and time. I said I'd give you space but I couldn't even muster up the courage to tell you to your face that I get weak when I see you. My stomach starts to turn and I get butterflies. Looking in your eyes, I get mesmerized. & I don't know where all of this comes from because there was a point in time when you meant nothing at all to me, and avoiding you was easy. Avoiding you meant I didn't have to deal with the fact that I was captivated by the look in your eyes from the day that I met you. Something about you. I didn't even like you at first. But something happened. Seemed every time you came around the world stood still for a moment. But now I'm so off balance and it's hard... this shit is so hard because the separation was finalized but now we have a whole new set of issues. We ultimately were our greatest downfalls and it's crazy to see the same fears and things that I was running from are now in my face and it's so confronting. It's so confronting and I can't breathe... I can't breathe... I can't breathe... but I must. Breathe in, breathe out... Let go.... Release. Damn.

I wrote this entry on August 18, 2018. At the time he and I had been riding heavy for 2 years. We danced this dance for 5 (nearly 6) years. There was a time when I would've done anything for him. I never wanted kids, but for him, I would have all his babies. I would've gone to the end of the Earth and back if he asked me to. I would have gotten hitched if he said, "Marry me." Like Mary J. Blige said in her song "Not Gon' Cry", "I would stop breathing if you told me to." He consumed me. He consumed my thoughts. He consumed my world. Actually...he *was* my world. I made him my everything. I was willing to put it all on the line. Our connection was so strong. At times it felt like he knew me better than I knew myself. He felt my energy. He sensed if I slept with another person. He sensed if I was in a bad head space. He sensed my joy, my pride, my excitement, and I, him... That's just how in tune we were. We'd finish each other's sentences. We were codependent. Depending on each other to *feel* good. Depending on each other to heal.

When I met him he was married, but separated from his wife. I didn't know initially, but I found out through a co-worker. Upon finding out and confronting him about it one night in the parking lot of what would then become our "spot", I pushed him to work things out with his wife. He couldn't understand why because he cared for me so deeply and he knew I cared for him too. He became my work husband and our bond grew intensely. He became my confidante, my friend, my lover, my everything. Our connection deepened overtime so much that eventually I wanted him all to myself. I was in love. Whenever I was around him, it's almost as if he sucked all of the air clear from my lungs with a straw. I would literally hold my breath. Every inch of my body tingled for him. Yearned for him. All I wanted was to make him happy even if that was at the expense of me. He consumed my thoughts. My nose was wide open and we only had sexual intercourse twice. I would perform oral on him in his car and I would swallow. So that energy he was exerting was being consumed right through my body. I absorbed him. When he sang, so did my heart. When he kissed me I'd melt. When he said I love you I believed him. When we'd go on dates and meet up at our spot, I felt like I was the most beautiful woman in the world. But he hurt me and I didn't know how to come back from that.

Us working together added a layer of difficulty. While there were no rules in the workplace prohibiting employees from dating each other, he developed a sense of paranoia despite the fact that we were always professional. I couldn't understand when he would push me away or try to pretend that his feelings weren't prevalent even though everyone around us could sense our connection. He wanted to keep us a secret. When I did something he didn't agree with or he got upset with me, he would withhold affection as a means of punishment. 5 whole years... 5 years of secrets, 5 years of sharing, 5 years of ups, downs, laughter, joy...pain. Waiting...hoping...yearning for a REALationship that never came. A REALationship based on mutual respect and commitment. At the time, my worth was dependent on whether or not he saw me. But how could he even see me, when I couldn't see myself?

Despite my willingness to do anything for him, there was one place I was reluctant to go. He wanted a threesome. When we attempted to do so in the car with one of his female friends, it didn't go well at all. I became jealous seeing him kiss another woman and I shut down the entire experience. Our dynamic changed after that. We became a bit distant from one another. He gaslit the fuck out of me. So much so that I felt like I was in the wrong. I felt like I couldn't trust him, and he felt like I was insecure. Even despite that experience, there was still a sense of entitlement to one another. The ultimate dagger to the heart was when I got guilt tripped into trying again, this time with one of my closest friends. I could hear my mom's voice saying, "Don't bring your friend around your man. Don't trust nobody!" But I pushed that voice in my head aside. We talked about doing it, and I even thought it could be a positive experience, but rather than wait for me to make the formal introduction in person and establish clear guidelines collectively, he took it upon himself to reach out to her and ask for sexual photos. She was honest and upfront with me and told me what happened. Admitted feeling uneasy about it and unsure if I would be okay with it, but what hurt the most was that against better judgment she still sent them. It was the ultimate betrayal and though it happened a couple of years ago, if I am to be completely honest, I still think about it from time to time. When I tried to confront him about it, he rushed me off the phone. The pain was agonizing. Two people who I loved dearly shattered my trust in a way that I never expected. I felt blindsided and completely gutted.

I loved him so much. But I knew I had to make a change. I declared that I would be moving to California before even securing a new job. I loved him so much that I moved across the country just to get away from him. My moving away was an act of resistance. A chance to prove to myself that I could live without him. But the problems still followed me. Despite that I had "moved on", having built a connection with someone else, he still found a way to try and exert control. When we'd speak to one another, we'd engage in regular conversation before he turned the conversation asking, "Who you fucking?" I never felt compelled to give a straight answer because honestly, it was the audacity for me. Despite my "moving on" I had to admit to myself that he was the thing that was in the way of me truly being present and allowing my new person to love me. Ultimately, it cost me a relationship.

I finally made a conscious choice to purge him completely from my life in October 2021. I asked a trusted male figure in my life to stand in place of him, so that I could say all of the things I never said to him. At first, I was hesitant. Hesitant because I fear disappointment. Hesitant because even though it wasn't him standing there, I've always held back from speaking up to him because he would get upset and withhold his love and affection from me as a form of punishment. My voice shook, my stomach rumbled, tears streamed down my face.

"All I wanted was to love you and you didn't know how to accept my love. You withheld your love from me when you got upset and I didn't deserve that. You fucking went after my friend! All I wanted was for you to love me. I have trouble letting love in because you made me feel like my love was never enough. You fucking piece of shit! I hate you! I hate you! I fucking hate you!" I screamed. I screamed. I screamed. I bent down and let out the loudest, piercing scream. "I fucking hate youuuuu!" Tears welled in my eyes and spilled out like water from a faucet. Snot oozed out my nose. I vomited mucus. My body suddenly felt weightless as I released everything that was inside of me. "Oh I hate you. I hate you. I hate you." I sobbed, allowing myself to be held and supported for the first time in my life. What's even more profound about this groundbreaking experience is that I had a doctor's appointment with my PCP earlier that day. I had told her that I had been feeling like I've had mucus at the base of my throat for years. She prescribed me something for post nasal drip, but after that purging, my throat has been completely clear. My throat chakra had been blocked for years because I held myself back from saying the thing that needed to be said. After that experience I blocked him from social media, blocked and deleted his number from my phone and I haven't looked back. 5 whole years...he doesn't get another second.

When we allow toxic people to keep us in a chokehold it becomes paralyzing. Blessings become blocked. Your life partner gets passed to the wayside. Actually, you're unable to see the good people that may be staring right in your face because you're so caught up on what's not even healthy for you. Take Ashanti's song "Foolish" as an example. She sings, "Baby why you hurt me? Leave me and desert me? Boy, I gave you all my heart and all you did was tear it up. Looking out my window, knowing that I should go. Even when I pack my bags, there's something that always holds me back."And hold me back it did. 5 years. Paralyzed. Unable to move past the chokehold he had on me because I felt like if I moved on, that would mean that I was unloyal. That would mean that I was not trustworthy. If I moved on, that would mean that I was abandoning him, just as I had been abandoned.

How many times must you go back to the person who is the source of so much pain? How hard does it have to hurt before you decide to make a change? What story are you telling yourself about your self-worth? Where does your value reside? It's so profound how even when we know we are in a toxic situation, we are drawn by it. We continue to go toward it even though we know it leads nowhere. Why do we put ourselves through so much hell and torture ourselves, accepting less than we deserve? My releasing the hold he had on me freed me up and allowed me to access my voice, stand in my power, and see myself for the first time as someone worthy to be loved, respected and honored. You holding this book in your hand and reading these words is a sign. A sign that it is time for you to take your power back. You've given away too much. **No more.**

A Practice:

Who is the person that has you stuck, unable to move past? Enlist the support of 2 trusted friends and one trusted male figure. Ask your trusted male figure to "stand in" place of that person who you just can't shake. What are the things you've held yourself back from saying? Tell that trusted figure. Don't hold back. Go all the way the fuck in and release all that's been on your heart. Yell if you need to, scream if you need to, cry if you need to. Once you're done, allow your support system to hold you.

Alternate Practice:

I acknowledge that not everyone has a support system that they feel 100% safe with to be completely vulnerable and naked in a real, raw way. If that practice is too intense for you, you can either:

1. Write a letter to that person saying all of the things that you've held inside. It doesn't matter if the letter is one page or 10 pages. Write it all out! When you're done, ball that shit up and throw it away. If you have a fire pit, burn it. That person doesn't get to have any more power over you. Feel your feels and cry your tears. It's all okay.
2. Draw that person's face, tape it to a wall and let it out! Yell it, scream it, release it. Rip that damn drawing up and toss it in the trash. Cry it out, drink some water, call a trusted person to get support. Then, when you're ready, deep breath in, deep breath out, place your hand over your own heart and feel the beat, acknowledging that you are Love and Pure Potential. Write a loving affirmation for yourself and post it somewhere where you can see it everyday.

An Affirmation:
I take back the key to my heart.
I unlock parts of me that I kept in the dark.
I find access to my own light.
My light is allowed to shine bright.

I am not the pain that I've endured. I am Light.

Chapter 15

Accountability

Allow Your Heart to Crack Wide the Fuck Open

My Story:

"*I create separation. It shows up everywhere in my life. It shows up in my love life. It shows up in my friendships. There's literally times where I won't leave my house for days and then it justifies the story that I am separate and alone. What I really want is connection.*" *I found myself standing in the training room of a leadership and self-development coaching program speaking on this. I went on to say, "There's a man that wants to love me and I am so afraid to let him in. I made him wait for 9 years before I let him get close to me. I'm going to let that man love me." The cheers and applause that I got from my teammates were the encouragement that I needed for me to go out and be open. I remember texting him later that night saying, "I know you're probably asleep, but I just wanted you to know that you're on my mind." As time went on I continued to practice vulnerability. I was able to heal so much hurt that I'd been holding on to that prevented me from allowing love in.*

One day when I was on the phone with him I told him that I realized all of the moments where I was closed off and I said, "I don't want to live like that anymore. I want to be open." I could feel him smiling through the phone as he replied, "Look at you being soft." I was never taught how to be soft. My mother lived her life closed, guarded, afraid to let love in, having experienced her own share of trauma in her life and romantic partnerships. Sometimes people come into your life to teach you something. From him I learned that it's okay to let my guard down, be loved and cared for. I learned that I can be in a relationship with someone. A relationship where I feel safe, yet that realization came a little too late. I found myself still feeling alone and this feeling of being alone has shown up so many times in my life as evidenced by all of my relationships that I've been in. The common factor was that I was with these men and something always came up missing. Either I didn't have the commitment, or I was in a situationship where we had all of the components of a relationship, but I wasn't worthy enough to have a title. I wasn't worthy enough to be taken on dates, shown around or loved out loud.

With him, it was like a blinding light. This was the final thing that I needed and it hit me like a boulder. I couldn't understand why after I finally decided to open up he wasn't being receptive, or taking advantage of the opportunity. I expected him to say, "This is my time. This is my chance. I'm never letting this woman out of my grasp." Why wasn't he matching that energy that he had in the beginning? I never realized that I drained him of all the energy he had. He didn't have the bandwidth to keep pursuing me. 9 years is a long fucking time and what I wanted was for him to grab me by the shoulders, look me in my eyes and say, "Stop fucking playing with me. You know you want this relationship. Drop the fear and trust." But that wasn't his job. I had been operating from my wounded self, not my healed self.

I didn't realize that I played a role in the breakdown, I know better now. I take full responsibility because I set it up this way from the beginning. He and I met in college, and when he and I reconnected years later after I saw him at a Uconn reunion cookout, I was adamant that I was moving to California and nothing and no one was going to get in my way. I didn't know how to say, "I care about you and I have entertained the thought of us being together, but I am afraid that when I move, you won't stay. I'm afraid that if I make this leap and follow my dreams, you won't go with me on the journey. I don't know if I'm worthy enough for you to uproot your whole life and do long distance with me." I was too afraid because to say all of that meant to let my walls down, be exposed and hold my heart in my hand, extending it out to him with no guarantee that he would be able to cherish, nurture and protect it. This fear existed even though he had shown me so much kindness, grace, and patience. He has a beautiful daughter and she's so young. He's a great father. I didn't believe that he would stay too far away from her. How could I make such a bold request? So anytime he mentioned the word girlfriend, I'd try and brush it off, even though deep down, I wanted to finally exhale and be cared for.

I think I always knew that deep down he and I were never meant to be together, but also I felt like I was running out of time. This idea of running out of time made me present to the fact that I was 30 years old and we may as well do this thing. Nevermind the fact that I fucking hate Jagged Edge's song "Let's Get Married" because they say, "We ain't getting no younger, so we might as well do it." Nevermind the fact that he and I were just two totally different people, in our own lanes. With the vision that I have for my life, I am not sure if he fits. This man came into my life and just shook everything up. Despite this, there were places he wasn't willing to go, because I created the space! Literally! I wanted flowers and dates, but I didn't want to give him my heart. I couldn't see the possibility of a long distance relationship because I had never seen an example of it. I kept my wall up because as mentioned before, the energy was lacking. The sex was great, but the energy to maintain a connection was fading with time. Back to feeling unhappy and alone. Resist, resist, resist. When I decided to try things out, the need that he once fulfilled no longer served me anymore.

As I began to heal, I realized that I always entertained dead end situations and I have always been romantically connected to someone consistently since high school. I never really took the time to sit down with Ashley. Learn Ashley. Get reacclimated with Ashley and what she likes. For the first time in my 31 years of life I decided to choose me this time. While it was heartbreaking to say the things I had been holding on to and hear from him the hard truths, I felt released. I could grieve and be with the sadness of the chapter closing, yet look forward with anticipation to all of the goodness that is in store for me. I get *to really be in a relationship with me from a place of goddamn peace. I get to lean into self-love, play, fun and creation. As a Life Coach who has a Coach I've taken on projects that are going to serve me and get me where I want to be in life, but the greatest project of them all is Me. I had been supporting other people so much in their healing that I forgot that Ashley still needed to heal and grow. In this moment I am grateful, and free. I get to create what an authentic, committed, safe, fun, exhilarating partnership looks like. Mmm! That is delicious...and I am ready.*

Let's be honest, none of us are saints. We are never going to get things one hundred percent perfect. Understand that sometimes you're the villain in someone else's story. Simply put, there will be moments when you're the toxic one and that's okay. I actually had the opportunity to reach out to a few of my exes and I asked them one question: what was my toxic trait? While one of the responses that I received told me how great of a person I was, there was one who had the courage to be honest. This was the guy that I treated as weak because I didn't feel like he was brave enough to protect me when we almost got robbed. He was afraid to share initially, but his response was super valuable. He said, "It was one trait that was coupled with another, if I remember. At the time, you were very codependent. Which led you to being possessive/controlling in the sense of having ALL my time, and when I would try to share that time around friends, you'd get upset when the focus wasn't just on you. It led me to feelings of guilt and having to lose out on some important moments in my friends' lives. But we were young and I wasn't necessarily great with confrontation or with expressing my feelings or points of view." I have it that there may be people in your own life, who've been impacted by you in the relationships, but didn't feel brave enough to share.

Have you taken accountability for the role you may have played in the breakdown of relationships? This is not to be confused with victim shaming or blaming. Though my intro was alluding to fuckboys, you gotta face the reality that sometimes you're the fuckboy, sis. Once you have the awareness, then you can change it. In the case of the gentleman in this chapter, I didn't think I was worthy, so I treated this man as if he wasn't worthy. Then I expected him to wait for me and jump on the opportunity to be with me 9 years after the fact. You may as well say 10 years because it was in the 10th year that I actually decided I was ready and healed enough to love him. Transformation can happen in an instant. Are you resisting it? Where has that gotten you? Are you satisfied with the results?

You get to decide, moment to moment, how you envision the next phase of your life. You can continue to be a victim and relive all of the old experiences of where you were hurt and why your mama did this or your daddy didn't do that, but it's time to woman up! You are a grown ass, capable ass, responsible ass woman. You don't have to live in the past. How are you showing up? Is that how you desire to live your life? My experience with him was a tipping point for me in that I drew a line in the sand. I decided from that moment that the days of settling were finished. I decided that I didn't want to live in a cycle of trauma. As mentioned, I knew deep down that I didn't see a future with this person, but I was trying to make it fit. I couldn't do it anymore. I couldn't waste his time, and I didn't feel like the train was moving. So I had to speak up and say, "I am no longer pursuing a relationship with you because I am unsure if you're able to love or show up for me in the way that I need you to." That took tremendous courage. Though in his response to me, he said I kind of missed that boat anyway, for the first time ever he and I were on the same page. Do you know how liberating that is? What is your tipping point?

A Practice:

Think of a time where you've displayed fuckboy behavior. Where you knew better, but absolutely did not do better. Where perhaps you may have been the one projecting your own hurt onto someone else. What was the outcome? What did that experience teach you? What do you commit to doing better moving forward? How are you granting yourself grace and compassion? If you want to take it one step further, you can reach out to a few exes and ask what your toxic trait was, but be prepared to just listen, not react. Just listen, say what resonates and thank them for their time. But if you ain't there yet, just do the reflection questions, Sis.

An Affirmation:
I am greater than the worst thing I've ever done.

Mistakes are meant to be learned from.

Chapter 16

Love After All

"Love is shown through actions. Stop making excuses for people who don't show up for you."
-Summer Walker

My Story:

Monday, November 1, 2021.

Mom: *"Have you talked to Trenna today?"*

Me: *"No, did something happen?"*

Mom: *"She's in Baltimore with Tray's family for his sister's birthday. I haven't heard from her all day. She didn't even say good morning. I called and texted both her and Tray and neither of them are answering me, and I'm worried."*

Mom: *"Trenna [is] in the hospital in critical condition."*

All of the air left my body and I could not breathe. The thought of my sister, my best friend somewhere hurt, fighting for her life left me in a state of paranoia that I'd never known. My beautiful sister and her life partner were hit by a drunk driver as they were walking back to their hotel between the hours of 2:30 and 3 am. My sister and her life partner, critically hurt. My sister's life partner, my future brother-in-law, dead. My sister, critical condition, trauma unit. My sister, fighting for her life. Broken femur, broken arm, broken hip, swelling in the brain, blood in the stomach, stroke, breathing tube, feeding tube. My sister, in critical condition, fighting ferociously for her life. My sister. My sister. My sister. Wait.. My future brother in law is dead?! No! No! No! No! No!

They had a love you could only hope for. A love that made you believe it was possible for you too. A love that was kinda sorta like R&B. A love where they could laugh, talk, enjoy one another's company, vibe, grow, build, progress. A love that was truly like home. A love, homegrown. A love that was ease. Sweet like honey. Where weekly date nights were a habitual thing. Where they were intentionally attempting to create a beautiful family. A love cut way too short. To say I was angry is an understatement. How could God finally show me a healthy example of what I could aspire to, only for it to be violently ripped away from my sister's grasp? How could she get to experience that beauty only to be left to navigate this world alone without her life partner? To return to an empty home they created. A life they built. Together. How? How? How? My heart shattered into a million pieces. My brother. My Taurus brother. My fam. Gone? Gone. Shock, in denial, peculiarity, eerie, numb.

This experience put a lot into perspective. This one precious life that we all have. How often we take it for granted. How often we think we have more time than we do. All it takes is one decision to change the trajectory of your life forever. One split decision impacting thousands. With this one precious life, do you really want to live it entertaining dead end situations that don't serve your highest and best? Dead end situations not nearly worthy of your greatness. Dead end situations that extract from your being. Dead end-

I had the opportunity to show up for my family in a way I hadn't done before. I was able to show up grounded. Rooted in love and an abundance of peace. Reminding my family that we are no good to others if we are not taking care of ourselves. Reminding them to keep praying for complete and total healing. Brain fully functioning, limbs and internal organs intact. My warrior goddess of a sister. A living, breathing, walking, talking miracle who will be able to use this story to inspire millions. My sister, a living testimony that God is able to do exceedingly and abundantly above all that we could ever ask or think. My sister. My warrior.

Monday, November 8, 2021, 5:36pm

Him: *Shares location: Baltimore VA Medical Center* Do you know where I can find something to eat in this area?

Me: In disbelief I say to my oldest sister and mom, "My friend drove to Baltimore... Wow."

Phone rings, Him: "Hey, I've been driving around but there's no parking in this area. Do you know where I can go to get something to eat around here?"

Me: "I am having dinner with my family right now. Where are you? You're here?"

Him: "I am here. Take all the time you need. I am going to go check into my hotel room now and maybe get something to eat through ubereats."

Me: "What hotel are you staying at?"

Him: "The Radisson."

Me: "Oh wow! That's the hotel our Lyft driver dropped us off at, but it turns out my hotel is connected to yours right on the corner. We're neighbors! I'll let you know when we get back to the hotel."

We hang up. My face, in complete awe and amazement.

This Morris Chestnut looking, waves spinning, smooth butter skin feeling, grande caffe mocha of a man drove 6 hours to be with me and show his support *for my family. This full, open hearted, vulnerable, strong, grown ass man who stood before me in the hotel lobby rearranged his whole schedule so he could be with me during a traumatic time in my and my family's lives. An upstanding, forward elevated, vibrate higher, book loving human being. He saw me as my masterpiece at a time where I was bare faced and naked, all the while being fully clothed in strength and perseverance. He. Showed. Up. Without me even having to ask. No excuses. No questions. He came. 6 hours. He drove.*

We embrace and sit in the lobby. Talking for hours. We laugh, we catch up, we reminisce. We drink from one another's energetic cup and pour into one another. We joke. We ascend higher, and higher, and higher. A literal love language. This quality time, talking about our lives, our hopes, our dreams. Exchanging resources and book recommendations. Speaking life into one another's visions and hopes for the world. Joking and baring it all. Being seen. Raw, vulnerable, free. We spend a few hours together. Going up to his room, watching crazy shows, we laugh.

We lie together in one another's arms. I feel safe here. What is this feeling? It's unfamiliar to me. I'm not used to this. I feel so…free. I ask him if I make him nervous. "No you don't make me nervous. I feel calm around you." Soft words, light, gentle touches, kisses that leave me feeling high. I am safe here. I fall asleep knowing I won't be harmed. A deep knowing that I could lay my burdens down. I feel ease. Accepting that I am worthy of someone showing up for me. Even if it's for a 6 hour drive here, a few hours of quality time and a 6 hour drive home. Safety. The one thing I searched for all my life. Safety. This man…Oh, God this man. Gratitude. Peace. Safety. Home.

I appreciate this man's friendship so much, because no matter the length of time we go without speaking, it is always love and appreciation. There's no pressure. I can be who I am. I can be as silly, or clumsy, or messy as I wanna be and it's okay. I truly believe that he was sent to me, to remind me that if a man truly cares about me, the **real** me, he will show up. No questions asked, no excuses, just action. This man was sent to me to reveal *in* me that I am worthy, not because of how great a performer I am, but that I am worthy simply because I exist. Prior to him showing up, I had made a decision that it was going to be a Me Season (shoutout to Issa Rae). That this was the time that I truly, *truly* leaned into self-love and being 100% committed to the process of being in relationship with me. I get to learn what I like and desire from a grown ass woman space. I get to step into the fullness of who I am. I get to take up space unapologetically. I get to be messy, vulnerable, raw, authentic and that is still enough! I am still enough!

Love is possible. Love is out there. I've seen it with my own eyes. I've heard its whisper. I've drank from love's fountain and girlaaa let me tell you!! It's so *sweet*. No more shrinking. No more settling. No more accepting less. You are more than that. Your life is bigger than entertaining small minds. If there's one thing you've learned from this book, my hope is that your key takeaway is that you don't have to suffer for love. You don't have to beg for it. You don't have to perform for it. You don't have to fight for it. Yes, you have to work for it, but you don't have to "get it out the mud." Full stop with that shit. You can be soft. You can take the armor off. I know that shit is heavy, sis. Let the armor fall. Put on the badass, powerhouse suit. You are a bad bitch. Own it!

A Practice:

Reflect on this: What are you pretending not to know about who you are? What mask are you hiding behind? Who told you that you couldn't ask for what you want, own all of your magic, and truly be great? You deserve it all. Can you see that? Can you see you? You are greater than your circumstances, more courageous than you know. If it needs to be a You Season, know that this is preparing you for who you are to become, and who is worthy to experience the full essence of your greatness. Breathe it in. Journal what comes up for you.

An Affirmation:
I am Madly in Love with Who I Am and Who I Am Becoming.
I am Dope As Fuck!

You deserve a love that doesn't involve suffering.

Until We Meet Again

You Get to Write the Next Chapter

Dear Sis,

I want to end with some grounding. I hope this book was as therapeutic for you as it was for me in the process of writing it. We're not going to get it 100%. We're going to have fuck ups. We're going to encounter many bumps in the road. We may make some human choices or give one too many chances. It is my hope that if you don't do anything else, *leannnnn* into self-love. *Leannnnnn* into your authenticity. Listen to the voice on the inside. Pay attention to the signs. Love the ones who treat you right and do away with the ones who don't. Understand that until you give yourself the loving care that you deserve, it's not going to make a difference whether a man comes into your life solid and wholesome or full of shit. You're not going to be able to be fully present in it until you treat you right. So let's ground ourselves in this:

You are divine. Your pure existence is so essential. Someone is praying to the Universe for the opportunity to know you. To love you. To cherish you. Your heart with every beat of that majestic organ flows from it, a sacred divinity. Breathe in joy. Breathe in self-trust. Breathe in self-love. Breathe in peace. Breathe in vulnerability. Breathe in light. Breathe in compassion. Breathe in beauty.

Breathe out hurt. Breathe out deception. Breathe out mistrust. Breathe out fear. Breathe out resentment. Breathe out old stories.

Today you write a new story. A story where you get to decide how you want the next phase of your life to go. A story where it is empowering, magical and real. Authentic. True. Valuable. Honorable. Special. Extraordinary.

I want you to picture your life one year from now. Who will you be? What will you create? What breakthroughs are available when you truly access your inner power? I can't wait to hear all about it. It's not going to be easy, Love. But it will be worth it. Embrace every aspect of the journey. Your healing starts now. It will get ugly. It will not always feel fun. But it's necessary. You are necessary. May you continue to snap out of the bullshit of limiting beliefs and dead end partnerships that no longer serve you and truly let that shit go. The time is now.

Go forth and be great.

With Love,

Your Best Friend in your Head, Your Life Coach, Your Sister, Your Mirror,

Ashley Burney

Your Final Declaration:

What do you want? Keep asking yourself this question and see what comes up. Then when you're ready, write your declaration for next year.

One year from now, I declare...

Acknowledgements

First and foremost, I want to thank God, creator of the Universe, for breathing life into me so that I could have the courage to live out my purpose of creating more joy, love, peace and authenticity in the world. I thank you for getting me through when the tough times came to take me out of the game. I thank you for providing and helping me see that so much is available to me. That I am abundant and divinely protected at all costs.

Immense gratitude to the brave women who were courageous enough to share their stories with me. It is an honor to have your full trust in allowing your stories to be heard. Whether you realize it or not, sharing your stories saved someone's life. Continue to lean into vulnerability and live in the fullness of who you are...a Masterpiece.

Thank you to my mom and father who chose to birth this greatness. You were already raising 5 children. You could've easily decided you didn't want another. I have it that you knew the 6th would be full of fire, passion, fierceness and a whole lot of power! Without you, there would be no me. I am truly grateful for every precious breath I get to take because of you.

Special thank you to my Life Coach, Kacey Cardin, who has always believed in me, pushed me, and saw my highest and best even when I didn't recognize it in myself. Thank you for always holding me high. Thank you for being a beautiful example of what it truly means to live your contract. You are light, power, passion, inspiration, beauty and grace. I love you forever.

Thank you to my family and friends who cheered me on, gave me feedback and loved the parts of me I thought were unlovable.

Thank you to all the fuckboys who lost me or passed me up, it sucks to be you. Ha! But seriously, may you tap into your own healing so you don't bleed on every partner you touch. May you choose growth even when it's uncomfortable so that you can raise healthy, wholesome and healed children.

For my Atlas Family of Choice (SF14), thank you for being the best team a woman can hope for. You've seen past the mask, and helped me to step into my power. Thank you for helping Wonder Woman take off the street clothes and burst out in full Wonder Women gear. Thank you for pushing me to take another step. Thank you for believing in me and trusting me with your vision. I love you all. For Justin and BT, thank you for taking my beautiful cover photos. Your artistic eye is incredible. To Lori, I hear your voice in my head everywhere, "Moment to moment." Thank you for seeing me. To Kimberlli for staying on my ass even when I pushed you away. You've always seen me. I love you, truly.

Thank you to my readers. You deserve a love that a person can't keep to themselves. You deserve to be loved out loud…& you will be.

Last, but certainly not least, I want to thank Me. I thank Me for stepping into my power, standing tall in my greatness and owning who I am– a Fierce, Passionate and Powerful Leader who doesn't shrink when circumstances arise. I step into it. I lean in. I get messy. I rise up again and again and again. I acknowledge Me for putting myself on the list, and truly believing that I can have it all: the love, the career, the peace and the freedom.

www.ingramcontent.com/pod-product-compliance
Lightning Source LLC
Chambersburg PA
CBHW070343010526
44119CB00029B/422/J